After
ETHNOS

After

ETHNOS

—

TOBIAS REES

Duke University Press   Durham and London   2018

© 2018 Duke University Press
All rights reserved
Printed in the United States of America on acid-free paper ∞
Designed by Courtney Leigh Baker
Typeset in Whitman and Myriad Pro by Copperline Books

Library of Congress Cataloging-in-Publication Data
Names: Rees, Tobias, author.
Title: After ethnos / Tobias Rees.
Description: Durham : Duke University Press, 2018. |
Includes bibliographical references and index.
Identifiers: LCCN 2018008240 (print) | LCCN 2018010132 (ebook)
ISBN 9781478002284 (ebook)
ISBN 9781478000617 (hardcover : alk. paper)
ISBN 9781478000808 (pbk. : alk. paper)
Subjects: LCSH: Anthropology. | Anthropology—Philosophy. | Ethnology.
Classification: LCC GN33 (ebook) | LCC GN33 .R44 2018 (print) |
DDC 301—dc23
LC record available at https://lccn.loc.gov/2018008240

Cover art: Étienne-Jules Marey, *Analysis of the Flight
of a Seagull*, 1887. Etienne-Jules Marey/Dépot du Collège
de France, Musée Marey, Beaune, France.

to my mother (1950–2012),

who escaped in her very own way(s).

———

and to J (2003) and C (2008),

whose lines of flight

I hope to follow

until my own final escape.

contents

what if ...

... what if the equation of anthropology, study of things human, with ethnog-raphy, the study and description of an ethnos, were a recent event? And what if one set out to undo this equation? If one were to cut loose the former from the latter?

Actually, what if one were to not only cut loose—liberate—anthropology from ethnos/ethnography/ethnology but also from "the human" *tout court*—from the in its aspirations time and place independent conception of the human as "Man" that first surfaced in the seventeenth century and that has since marked the con-dition of possibility of the human sciences (chief among them anthropology)?

What would—what could—an anthropology after ethnos / after "the hu-man" look like? What if ...?

acknowledgments

This much I learned: Every relation one has, offers a singular possibility to actualize one's being—one no other relation can offer. The powerful implication of this observation is that it is through relations that one is in the world. No relations, no self. Acknowledgments, then, the maps of relations they are, are akin to a map of one's history of being, of being in the world.

IT IS AN EXTRAORDINARY honor—a joy—to acknowledge the different relationships that have been constitutive of my being in the world (with the world) that have made this book possible.

The first time the idea for a book on anthropology after ethnos occurred to me was on an extremely cold Montreal winter day, in a terribly overheated room, where Dörte Bemme, Raad Fadaak, Kristin Flemons, Fiona Gedeon Achi, and Julianne Yip kept insisting that I better explain the difference between ethnography and fieldwork. Why would this difference matter for anthropology? What does "after ethnos" mean? How could one even fathom anthropology beyond culture and society? Or after the human? These were the early days of our thought collective. Adam Fleischman later joined us.

I want you all to know that I can't quite put in words the gratitude I feel for our clandestine conversations, for your complicity, for your challenges and your care, for your friendship. Your questions—and your visits—sustained me, sustained my sense of self. And your encouragements gave me the hope that some of the ideas that I found myself intrigued by could matter. I add that none of these ideas would have assumed the form they assume in this book without you.

Thank you.

Of similar importance was the friendship—and mentorship—of George Marcus. George, more than anyone else, has encouraged me to distinguish fieldwork from ethnography (from the field-based study of an ethnos). George and I are working together on an edited volume on fieldwork after ethnos that I hope will soon be published—as a document of our friendship, as an exploration of possibilities that exceed whatever I write in this book.

I also want to mention here my heartfelt gratitude to Setrag Manoukian: your sense of poetry often carried me—and the elegant ease with which you render visible beauty in the unexpected often provided me with a shelter. I wish I had told you more often. And earlier.

Without Mara Eagle, without our countless conversations, the flights taken in this book would lack the wild intensities that only Mara can give to things. Our atlas project is the future.

I had the extraordinary fortune that friends near and far found *After Ethnos* provocative enough to organize podium discussion and workshops about the book when it was still in a manuscript state: George Marcus at UC Irvine; Vincanne Adams, Ian Withmarsh, and Sharon Kaufman at UCSF; Nancy Chen at UCSD; Mette Nordal Svendson at Copenhagen; Janet Roitman, Nikolas Langlitz, and Miriam Ticktin at the New School; and Johannes Quack and Sandra Bärnreuther in Zürich.

Thank you for inviting me, for providing me with the opportunity to discuss the ideas outlined here with you and your colleagues, and for exposing me to your exceptional students who derailed me and caught me off foot more than once.

I also had the great fortune to discuss the manuscript—or some of the ideas contained therein—with Lawrence Cohen, Peter Redfield, Stephen Collier, Janina Kehr, Ellen Hertz, Townsend Middleton, Stefan Helmreich, Gregor Dobler, Laura Emdal Navne, Mie Seest Dam, Iben Mundbjerg Gjødsbøl, Katherine Lemons, and Yves Winter.

Fiamma Montezelomo has been an unfailing guide: Her words of wisdom and her calls to arms carried me when everything seemed to fail.

Ian Withmarsh read several versions of the manuscript. And Ian's readings not only made the manuscript much better, he also encouraged me more than anyone else to push the implications and to follow them.

Paul Rabinow has been there (almost) since the start. As everyone who can read can see: I owe him more than I can put in words. He was the first to teach me that anthropology is more than ethnography—and he was the first who pushed me to explore my own lines of thinking. Our ongoing work of freedom means the world to me.

I would also like to thank Fritz W. Kramer, who encouraged me to state loud and clear that classical modern ethnography is a matter of the past—just like classical modern art or classical modern architecture; Allan Young, for our daily conversations about an intellectually oriented anthropology; and Abe Fuks, for everything.

At Duke University Press I want to thank Elizabeth Ault, Stephanie Gomez Menzies, Sara Leone, and two anonymous reviewers, whose encouraging and questioning comments greatly improved the manuscript. Above all, however, I want to thank Ken Wissoker, whose care for author and text is of a kind that I have never experienced before: Ken read, Ken replied, Ken directed, Ken intervened, Ken suggested. Thank you indefinitely, Ken, for taking me seriously, for engaging me, for providing orientation, for taking me on.

Alberto "Willi" Sanchez and Tarek Elhaik are my best friends in the world. As Cicero knew: "Virtue creates the bond of friendship and preserves it. For in her is fidelity; and when she has raised her head and shown her own light in another, she moves towards it and in turn receives its beams; as a result love or friendship leaps into a flame; for both words are derived from a word meaning 'to love.' But love is nothing other than the great esteem and affection felt for him who inspires that sentiment."

I love you.

Above all hovers my family, dead and alive. No relations, no self: you are my life. From beginning till end. Thank you. Thank you for everything.

— all of it —

Today, what is anthropology?

For most of the twentieth century, most anthropologists understood themselves as ethnographers. The art of anthropology, that was the careful, fieldwork-based description of faraway others—of how social structures secretly organized the living together of a given society, of how a people had endowed the natural world surrounding them with cultural meaning.

While the poetics and politics of ethnography changed dramatically over the course of a century, the basic equation of anthropology with ethnography remained so evident, so obvious, that the possibility of questioning it occurred to hardly anyone.

But today?

Beginning in the late 1990s, new, unanticipated lines of research have emerged that have little—in some cases nothing—in common with anthropology defined as ethnography, that is, the fieldwork-based study of an *ethnos* (Greek for "a people"). The idea for this book grounds in the observation that one, perhaps unintended, effect of at least some of these new lines of research has been that they silently differentiated anthropology from ethnography—as if they differentiated a curiosity about the human from the fieldwork-based study of ethnos, of territorially imagined societies and their culture or social structure, their symbols and rituals and structures of belief.

After Ethnos is an attempt to bring the dissociation of anthropology from ethnography into view. It is an attempt to rethink anthropology—*all of it*—from the perspective of the "after." What is more, it is an attempt to increase the intensity of the turbulences, the trouble that the after triggers. And it is an attempt to make available (at least some aspects of) the new/different anthropologies "after ethnos" it has allowed for.

— escapes (always) —

After Ethnos is a nonprogrammatic book.

My aim is not to argue that all of anthropology is "after" ethnos. Nor do I mean to suggest that there is a new, still emergent formation—the anthropology after ethnos. I have not sought to provide a programmatic statement of what an anthropology after ethnos—after ethnography, culture, society, place—might look like. Much of anthropology continues to revolve around just these concepts. Rather, the ambition (if this is not too ambitious a term) of *After Ethnos* is to look for escapes from the already thought and known, from scripts. My goal has been to look for opportunities to break free, to depart, to leave behind, to derail, to undermine. *After Ethnos* is about (the possibility of) lines of escape. The various escapes the book offers go in different, perhaps even mutually exclusive, directions.

However, I do not look for ways to go (arrive) somewhere.

— the human (deanthropologized) —

It was only very gradually that I began to understand that the differentiation of anthropology from ethnos also leads to a dissociation of anthropology from the human, that is, with the abstract, time- and place-independent figure of "Man" that was invented and stabilized in Europe between the 1630s and the 1830s and that has marked the historical condition of the possibility of a discipline called *anthropology*.

Culture, society, history, language, suffering, nation, meaning, symbol, ritual, myth, nature, subjectivity, the body: What if all the concepts anthropologists have relied on, however implicitly, to stabilize "the human," to set it apart, to create a separate human reality that would require its own science (anthropology), were actually inventions of a recent European past rather than human universals on which one would build "anthropological" knowledge?

Could one rethink anthropological research as the continuous practice of *deanthropologizing* anthropology? As an effort to let fieldwork accidents give rise to surprises in which humans—and anthropology and bacteria and robots and landscapes and snails and much more—are released from "the human"?

Not once and for all, as if there were some better, truer ontology waiting elsewhere (I am not an ontologist), but time and time again?

After Ethnos is an effort to think out loud about these questions. What is more, it is an attempt to wonder if anthropology could be a form of inquiry— an art—that always seeks to exceed its own condition of possibility.

— fieldwork (itself) —

After Ethnos is also an effort to differentiate fieldwork—understood as a technique of immersion into everyday life, as a methodological opportunity to let accidents give rise to the unanticipated—from ethnography, that is, from the fieldwork-based study of an ethnos.

———

I am an anthropologist, but not an ethnographer. I conduct fieldwork—but not ethnography.

———

Why and to what ends does one conduct fieldwork when one is not—no longer—conducting ethnography? What is fieldwork itself? What is its object— if any?

— form (exposure) —

When I then sought to enroll others in the project of imagining anthropologies after ethnos / the human, I ran into vehement—at times furious—critique.

Why would you abandon ethnos? Why culture and society? Are you a neoliberal? What is your politics? Why do you emphasize thought and philosophy? Isn't this anthropocentric? Don't these concepts transport the worst of the nineteenth century—reason, big white men, elitism, parochialism, colonialism? Why do you speak of the emergent? What is the aim of your focus on the new/different? Doesn't your approach reflect a modernist, linear philosophy of time? Why—and to what ends—would one study movement or the "always new"? What would that even mean? Doesn't space matter?

I found the questions troubling, the vehemence with which they often were articulated unsettling. Until, at one point or another, I began to understand that the reason for the critique I faced was not my project as such—not the push toward the "after"—but that my language, the vocabulary that I had available for myself (in many ways a reflection of the places of my education and thus of chance rather than of design) could not accommodate the anthropologies after ethnos / the human my critiques envisioned.

Differently put, I began to understand that the stakes of the "after" I sought to make available exceeded the vocabulary of possibilities I had relied on to make the after visible.

When I began to write up *After Ethnos*, I was determined to preserve—or capture—as much of that which exceeds me as I could. How, though? How to capture that which exceeds oneself? The response I eventually came up with I think of in terms of exposure: I wrote the first chapter, *on anthropology (free from ethnos)*, presented it on multiple occasions (some formal, many more informal)—and then meticulously documented (often times taped) the comments and challenges I found myself confronted with. Once back home, I worked through these challenges, time and again, baffled, angry, surprised, happy—until a set of texts emerged, texts that carry me into uncharted territories, that is, into terrains in which my initial language fails (or is challenged), failures (challenges) that give contours to stakes I wasn't aware of when I set out to write. The outcome is a set of responses—of differentiations—that run somewhat diagonal to the arguments I offer in chapter 1, that explore its stakes differently (from different vantage points).

Next I wrote chapter 2, *"on" the human (after "the human")*. I repeated the same process—exposure, taping comments/conversations, working through them, writing texts that would give contour to that which exceeded my initial formulations—while keeping in mind what I learned when I wrote the texts following chapter 1. Then came chapter 3, *on fieldwork (itself)*, and eventually chapter 4, *on the actual (rather than the emergent)*.

Each chapter, thus, is followed by a series of digressions—some short, others not exactly short—and differentiations that were triggered by the critical interventions of friends and interlocutors.

The final product is an untamed book, exuberant, provocative, fierce, funny (or so I hope), and always looking for lines of escape.

After Ethnos, while written by me, (hopefully) exceeds me in multiple ways.

What is anthropology once it is differentiated from ethnos?

What is anthropology when one gives up the once constitutive interest in spatially coded differences? If one bids farewell to culture, society, territory?

What is anthropology when one breaks not only with "the human" but as well with the idea that there is a separate human reality—humans as more than mere nature, as culture and/or society—that demands its own kind of science? When one breaks with the human without assuming that beyond the human there is some other, some truer reality? Without assuming that beyond the human lays some saving moral ground (nature)? That is, when one rejects ontology (or ontologies)?

Can an anthropology "after the human" be practiced at all?

What is fieldwork after it has been decoupled from ethnography? Is fieldwork the only form anthropological research can take?

Why and to what ends does one conduct anthropology after ethnos/the human? What is the purpose? Truth? Knowledge? Of what?

Today, what is anthropology? What is anthropological?

on anthropology

(free from ethnos)

What is it all about? What is anthropology?
What is anthropology's job? What's its domain?
. . . I don't know what anthropology . . . is,
but I don't think that it is or should be defined as ethnography.
DAVID SCHNEIDER, *Schneider on Schneider.*

ONE

In retrospect it seems as if the ethnographic project of classical modernity came to an end at one point in the late 1990s. I write "in retrospect" because the passing away of anthropology in its form of classical modern ethnography was—awkward as this may sound—an unintended effect, an accident. As it was unintended, no one had been waiting for it, and so it could be recognized only in hindsight—in "retrospect"—and not without surprise and even sadness.[1]

Already in the 1970s the ethnographic project as it was envisioned by Adolf Bastian and Friedrich Ratzel in Germany; by Franz Boas in the United States; by Alfred C. Haddon, William H. R. Rivers, Alfred R. Radcliffe-Brown, and Bronisław Malinowski in Great Britain; and by Émile Durkheim, Marcel Mauss, Paul Rivet, and Lucien Lévy-Bruhl in France had come under severe critique. The purpose of this critique was not to bring ethnography to an end.

The goal of the various critical voices that had begun to emerge in a systematic, accumulative fashion since the late 1960s was to improve—poetically as well as politically—the ethnographic documentation of those faraway others that anthropologists had begun to systematically study at the turn of the nineteenth to the twentieth century.[2] It was meant to correct what seemed to many to be the "mistakes" of the great ethnographers of the past.[3]

For the purpose of my argument, there is no need to retrace here the intricate ways in which the many different kinds of inner-disciplinary critique developed over time; it suffices instead to provide a sketch of the one line of critique that marked, at least from the retrospective point of view from which I write, the beginning of the (unintended) end of classical modern ethnography, the critique of the philosophy of history on which ethnographers had relied since the late eighteenth century.[4]

———

"Classical modern ethnography has come to an end."

What does it take for this sentence to sound as obvious and as uncontroversial as if one were to say, "Classical modern painting has come to an end"?

Is the end of classical modern ethnography really controversial?[5]

TWO

In Europe, the second half of the eighteenth century brought what one could refer to as the "temporalization" of the spatial differences of life forms. It was a period during which the number of travel accounts that provided reports of foreign forms of human existence—whether from the past or from elsewhere—significantly increased, leaving interested observers with the baffling question of how one could make sense of this bewildering diversity.[6]

The *philosophes* of the Enlightenment approached this challenge by way of inventing a new, previously unknown genre of scholarly literature, *history*. Authors as diverse as Voltaire, Turgot, Condorcet, Kant, Ferguson, and Herder (and many in their aftermath) began writing the first histories of "mankind" that were arranging the people of the world along a single axis that led from those others who were "still" living *ab originem* (the premoderns, "living fossils" as Edward Burnett Tylor would later famously call them) to those Europeans who had "already" progressed through history and hence were at home in the here and now (the moderns).

For the coming into being of anthropology, the emergence of history—and of the singular collective called humanity that was the imagined author of history—was a decisive event: the emphatic distinction between premoderns and moderns humans brought about the condition of the possibility of the field of study that late eighteenth-century authors began to refer to as "ethnography"—a field of study defined by its modern expert knowledge of those who were still living in the premodern past (for a history of the term ethnography see chapter 3).

Ethnography emerged as the "science" of the people without history, without state, without science—of those "still" living in a cosmos, with mythical structures, magic, and rituals.

The critiques of the 1970s and 1980s observed that many of the twentieth century ethnographers—even though they had long moved against the very idea of the "primitive" or the "premodern"—were ultimately still relying on the distinctions invented by eighteenth-century European philosophers: as long as they described the other with words like "cosmos," "myth," "ritual," "kinship systems," and "magic"—all markers of a past—they were ceaselessly reinscribing the temporal distinction between "them" and "us" they had set out to critique. As long as the ethnographic project was conceived of in terms of classical modernity, there seemingly was no possibility to escape the predicament: anthropology was and continued to be contingent on the philosophy of history.[7]

What was one to do?

The dominant response to what Johannes Fabian called the "denial of coevalness" (Fabian 1983)—the active effort, on behalf of ethnographers, to locate the friends they have found in "the field" in the past—was the effort to find ways of anthropological inquiry and ethnographic writing that would lead ethnography beyond the great divides of modernity. One important approach to this challenge was to write historical ethnographies, carefully documenting the long "world historical" involvement of other societies (thereby undermining the myth of the "timeless other").[8]

Another significant approach designed to achieve coevalness was the effort to find ways of integrating concrete others into ethnographic texts—by way of naming friends one has found in the field, by way of giving space to their "voices," by way photography and co-authorship. Self-consciously, ethnographers began experimenting with new forms of writing ethnographies—an "experimental moment" that led to a wave of reflective, polyphonic, dialogic, and other forms of ethnographic texts.[9]

In the shadow of these two dominant approaches—both of which, despite their critical intent, were affirming the very idea of the classical ethnographic project (they were meant as improvement)—a small group of anthropologists opted for an altogether different approach for leading anthropology beyond the temporal dilemmas so deeply inscribed in the idea of ethnography. And while this "third way" was initially hardly influential, it quickly gained a dynamic of its own—a powerful dynamic that was to lead anthropologists away from their established preoccupations and into thoroughly new terrains, empirically as well as conceptually.

For so many years, or so one could summarize the argument of this "third way" in retrospect, ethnographers have tried to convince the world that the primitive is not primitive, that the Other is not timeless, that "we" are "contemporaries," and nobody listened. So maybe it would now make sense to go ahead and ask, "Have we ever been modern?"

In order to convey a sense of the critical ethos that informed this question in the mid-1980s, I cite a passage from Paul Rabinow's contribution to *Writing Culture* (Marcus and Clifford 1986): "We have to anthropologize the West. We have to show how exotic its constitution of reality has been: emphasize those domains most taken for granted as universal; make them seem as historically peculiar as possible; show how their claims to truth are linked to social practices and have hence become effective forces in the social world."[10]

In the mid- to late 1980s there were fairly different ways of taking up this call to "anthropologize the West." Some took it to mean an ethnographically grounded critique of the hegemony and ideology of Western science and medicine; others believed it suggested that the institutions constitutive of our presumed modernity (science, technology, political economy, medicine) are as culturally peculiar, as socially constructed, as myth and ritual; and yet others embraced it as a suggestion to carefully study the "modern" as a distinct form of reasoning.

Recall Bruno Latour's *Nous n'avons jamais été modern*—first published in 1991 (in English in 1993)—and you see the synergetic coming together, in the late 1980s and early 1990s, of anthropology, critical theory, the sociology of scientific knowledge, science studies, literary critique, feminism, cultural studies, and medical anthropology (Latour 1991, 1993).

————

Of course, humans existed before the late eighteenth century—but the human is a distinctive eighteenth-century formation (see chapter 2). And, of course, humans were telling histories long before the eighteenth century. The argument here is not that humans were ignorant about the differences between past and present. However, most of these histories had been—and continued to be—local stories, that is, histories of local groups and people. A universal history of humanity, of humanity as such (and humanity is a concept—a collective—that was unknown before the turn from the eighteenth to the nineteenth century), from its earliest emergence at some point in the past to the present is a distinct product of the second half of the eighteenth century. And many of the key categories that anthropology has historically relied on to describe its object of analysis emerged alongside this universal history—culture, humanity, history, morals, body, nation, primitive, progress, race, society. Most of these concepts were unknown previously—or they assumed entirely new meanings.

THREE

Perhaps there is no need here to delve into the intricacies of inner-disciplinary developments or to trace how the first, still somewhat awkward "ethnographies of the West" gradually gave rise, via detours, to anthropology as it is practiced in today's major research departments (at least in North America). It suffices instead to note, first, that at one point in the late 1980s or early 1990s a number of anthropologists began to enter—per fieldwork—domains that were formerly believed to be beyond the scope of anthropological expertise or interest, most notably (but by no means exclusively) medicine, science, and technology.[11] And, second, that what was at first a quite "exotic" enterprise, at least by the standards of classical ethnography, namely the anthropologist in the laboratory, soon became one of the most important and innovative fields of anthropological research—the anthropology of modernity, of science, medicine, media, the Internet, finance, technology, and much more (at home and afar).

The effect of this growth in unexpected directions has been a far-reaching—still ongoing—metamorphosis of anthropology; it led, especially on the level of a new generation of anthropologists that was no longer educated in traditional terms and no longer conducted classical fieldwork, to the emergence of a thematically new kind of anthropology, one thoroughly removed from classical modern ethnography and its interests in segmentary lineages, gift exchange, and mythic structure (all topics that, together with the study of rituals, still dominated anthropology in the 1970s and early 1980s and that are largely absent from today's journals).[12]

A sense of just how far-reaching the metamorphosis anthropology has been undergoing is, is conveyed by the controversies that surround the attempts to revise the intellectual tool kit of the discipline that the new anthropology has brought about.[13] These revisionisms (plural) are the direct result of the observation that "the old" concepts and tools—namely those anthropology provided to those who set out to study ethnos, its culture, its kinship structures, its economy, mode of subsistence, political systems, and religion—seemed less than useful for studying and analyzing "the new" domains anthropologists had entered.

How does one study an HIV epidemic? And how science? What is interesting about, say, adult cerebral plasticity? And what about neoliberal city planning? Or the emergence of transnational companies? Or CO_2 bubbles in ice that were frozen for millions of years and that are now released? Or cheese making? Or Hurricane Katrina?

In the late 1990s anthropology was entering an open situation, a situation full of passionate disagreement, of regret, of polemic as well, but also of the clear sense that there was a need for innovations: new research domains brought about the need to articulate new forms of anthropological curiosity, new tools, new ways of thinking about and designing research.[14]

Arguably, anthropologists are still experimenting with such tools, curiosities, and research designs—and amid their experimentation they recognized (some surprised, others simply sad) that the ethnographic project of classical modernity had ceased to exist.[15]

What began as a response to the temporal dilemma built into classical modern ethnography had become a project thoroughly decoupled from precisely this classical modern ethnography.

FOUR

One of the most exciting intellectual effects of the decoupling of anthropology from classical modern ethnography has been (or so I dare say) the emergence of the possibility of a "philosophically inclined anthropology." In order to specify what I mean by this clumsy phrase—a philosophically inclined anthropology—and to clarify in what sense its becoming possible has been an effect of the decentering of the classical ethnographic project, I would like to contrast the concept of "anthropology" that it advances with the comprehension of anthropology that was built into modern ethnography (for it is precisely on the level of conceptualizing anthropology—what it is, what its challenge is—that the philosophically inclined variant has been an event).

What from the perspective of classical modern ethnography, did the term "anthropology" refer to?

If one addresses this question to the works that have shaped twentieth-century anthropology—from Rivers to Malinowski or Radcliffe Brown to Turner, from Boas and Benedict to Mead and Geertz—a perhaps surprising but consistent picture emerges: In its form of classical modern ethnography, anthropology has been much less concerned with *anthropos* (Greek for "the human") than with *ethnos*. Ethnographers, it turns out, have never really asked *Was ist der Mensch?*[16] No, the question that has nourished their curiosity, that drove them to conduct research and that animated their debates was not the question concerning the human but rather the question what forms human living together could take. And the reason for this focus on ethnos rather than anthropos is that they ultimately took it for granted that the question concerning the human had long been answered: If anthropology assumed the form of ethnography then because ethnos, ultimately, was the answer to the question concerning anthropos. Most clearly this taken for grantedness comes into view when one turns to the two most prominent "answers" that have stabilized anthropology qua ethnography, "society" and "culture."

Humans, or so "social" anthropologists have argued, are "social" beings. Wherever one turns, they live in a "society" and whatever they do is embedded in and shaped by societal patterns: Nothing "human" can exist outside of things social. The challenge faced by the social anthropologist, consequently, is to travel the world and to ethnographically document, on the one hand, the various forms societies may take (ideally working toward an inventory of these forms), and to show, on the other hand, that a proper comprehension of these forms is the true key for understanding how humans live and think and exist in the world.

In a similar (and yet so different) way, "cultural" anthropologists have taken it for granted that humans are—what else?—"cultural" beings. They have taken it for granted, that is, that what distinguishes humans, what sets them apart, is their capacity (pace Marvin Harris and cultural materialism) to endow themselves and their surroundings with meaning. Indeed, as the cultural anthropologist sees it, nothing humans can do or think of exists without meaning—be it in complex rituals or in a simple experiment. Even the very idea of "society" (or so the "cultural" critique of "social" anthropology goes) is ultimately a cultural category, is meaning.[17] It follows that the challenge faced by the cultural anthropologist—who is equipped with the certainty that whatever she will find, however bizarre, is culture—is to travel the world, to ethnographically document foreign "cultures" and show that a proper comprehension of the "web of meaning" that is constitutive of a culture is the true key for understanding how humans "are" elsewhere.[18]

For social and cultural anthropology the question is not—and never was—*Was ist der Mensch?* but rather *What forms can society and culture take?*

The possibility of what I have suggested to call a philosophically inclined anthropology (after ethnos) opens up precisely where the answers on which anthropology in its form of ethnography has relied—on which it has been built its house of knowledge—fail and assume the form of a question.[19]

Take, for example, "culture." When did "culture"—the suggestion that humans are more than mere nature, that they live in a distinctive human sphere of innovation that demands its own science—become a convincing answer to the question concerning the human? Arguably "culture" is not a timeless category. It was not always around, has not always and at all times been central to thinking about things human. "Culture," this is to say, has a history and is a place-specific category of thinking about humans in the world (the term culture was first used to conceptualize humans—the place of humans in the world—in the late 1770s, by Johann Gottfried Herder).

———

On the surface of things "culture"—or "society"—may seem to be a neutral, analytical term. However, this seemingly neutral analytical term silently transports an eighteenth-century conception of humans as more than mere nature that might be entirely inadequate to the present. For example, in the age of anthropogenic climate change, would one really want to be a *cultural* anthropologist?

———

The possibility of the field of research I have described as a philosophically inclined anthropology opens up precisely where given anthropological ways of defining the human—culture, society/the social, history—lose their evidence: where they get cracks, however subtle, where they begin to produce questions rather than answers, where they become a problem, rather than a solution.

If humans were not always "cultural," if there once were conceptually—epistemologically and ethically—different ways of being human in the world, then couldn't it be that there are instances in the here and now that escape the conceptualization of the human implicit in the culture concept (or in the concept of society/the social)? Instances that open up new, different, yet unknown, possibilities of being human? Ones no one has ever seen or heard of?[20]

If there was a before or, indeed, many different kinds of before, then couldn't there also be an after? Or many different kinds of after? Each with its own, distinctive line of flight?

Where the classical ethnographer begins with an answer—culture, society—and then travels the world and decodes the life forms she finds in terms of her answer (ceaselessly reducing others to her own concepts), the philosophical anthropologist (of thought—and the human—in motion) is curious to find out if, today, other possibilities of thinking the human exist or are coming into existence, possibilities that in their conceptual specificity escape the conceptual grid of our already established ways of thinking and knowing things human, that undermine their self-evidence and thereby open up new—hitherto unthought of—spaces of being (which are to be explored by way of fieldwork and research).

Where social and cultural anthropology always only find more of the same—for all there is and ever will be is culture and society—the philosophically inclined anthropologist finds herself confronted with a question. Or better: with a set of questions, questions that the old answers cannot tame anymore.

From the perspective of the philosophically inclined anthropology I seek to outline here, modern ethnography is an intellectually (and ethically) highly problematic enterprise. It keeps the doors firmly locked, which the philosophically inclined anthropologist (of thinking) is ceaselessly pushing wide open; it shuts out the possibility that "elsewhere" it could be "different," where the philosophically inclined anthropologist is busy exploring precisely this possibility, curious to know/learn if yet unthought of ways of answering (and posing) the question concerning the human are coming into existence.

The philosophically inclined anthropology has opened up a vast new space of research curiosities and possibilities where before there simply was—nothing.

FIVE

What one may call the disciplinary significance of the coming into existence of the possibility of a philosophically inclined anthropology is that it has allowed (at least some) leaving behind the dilemmas anthropologists have struggled with ever since they have entered new terrains—the fact that neither their established objects (societies and cultures) nor their taken for granted decoding tools (society and culture) are helpful for understanding the new phenomena and constellations they are confronted with.

———

Isn't it curious how in classical modern ethnography the *explanans* and the *explanandum*, the thing to be explained and the thing that explains, are one?

———

Is avian flu a cultural category? Is the Internet a social fact?[21]

For the philosophically inclined anthropologists these questions are of no significance. As they don't define anthropology as the study of "society" or "culture," they are liberated from what appears from afar as the desperate effort to adjust the concepts of "society" or "culture" in such a way that one may "anthropologically" study, for example, avian flu or the Internet.

The decoupling—the liberation—of anthropology from ethnography/ethnos has opened up the possibility of a different kind of anthropology, one that is neither focused on society nor on culture but on "thought" and the curious figure that has once been called "Man."

Are new ways of answering (or posing) the question concerning the human emerging today? In what areas? In yeast biology? In drosophila genetics? In behavioral dog genomics? In avian flu research? In HIV vaccine research? In the study of adult neurogenesis? Where, and in which ways, do we see the *humanum* in motion, in metamorphosis?[22]

Perhaps one can see now why I call this a "philosophically inclined *anthropology*." It rearticulates anthropology in anthropological terms; it is focused on the human and on thought rather than on culture or society.[23]

And perhaps one can also see why I call it a "*philosophically* inclined anthropology." It is philosophical to the degree that it is a variant of the critical work of thought on thought that is guided by the effort to find out—by way of fieldwork and research—how and to what extent it might be possible (or it has become possible) to think differently.[24] To be a philosophically inclined anthropologist is to orient oneself in thinking by way of thinking—in order to find out if, and if, then in what concrete ways new venues of thinking/being are coming into existence.[25]

It is only a slight exaggeration—and a retrospective one—to say that in the last two decades (since the late 1990s) anthropology has been liberated from the dominance of ethnography—from the focus on ethnos, society, and culture. And this liberation has brought about a condition of possibility for practicing anthropology in anthropological (rather than ethnos-graphic) terms.[26]

As if it were an empirically inclined, fieldwork-based philosophy.[27]

anthropology and philosophy (differently)

I anticipate critique.

"But the encounter between anthropology and philosophy is hardly a new one. Anthropologists have conversed with philosophers for a long time!"

I concede. Anthropologists and philosophers have conversed for a long time. But I would want to add two clarifying observations about form and content of this long-standing exchange.

First, the overwhelming majority of the discussions between anthropologists and philosophers were grounded in the taken-for-granted, mutually shared understanding of anthropology as ethnography. The role assumed by the anthropologist vis-à-vis the philosopher—call it the division of labor that structured their exchanges—was that of the expert of not yet modern societies and cultures.

Second, almost all of the conversations between anthropologists and philosophers have revolved around two themes only. On the one hand, there were discussions about the difference between "primitive" and "modern" modes of thought, and, on the other hand, there were discussions about the universal existential grounds of what it means to be human, across time and space.

What I have suggested to call a philosophically inclined anthropology departs from both form (the equation of anthropology with ethnography) and content (the two themes around which the conversation revolved). And it is precisely this departure that creates the condition of the possibility for anthropology to become itself philosophical: to curiously and courageously enter the terrain formerly left to the philosophers.

Let me explain.

primitive thought

It has arguably been the most persistent question that anthropologists and philosophers have discussed with one another—the question whether or not "primitive thought" differs in kind from "modern thought." The origins of this question lay in a little known disagreement between Lucien Lévy-Bruhl (1857–1939) on the one hand and Émile Durkheim (1858–1917) and his nephew, Marcel Mauss (1872–1950), on the other. To be more precise, it lay in Lévy-Bruhl's subtle provocation of Durkheim and Mauss.

Throughout the nineteenth century, philosophers and anthropologists took it for granted that the categories of thought that organize the human mind were no different among "the primitives" and "the moderns." While there was wild disagreement among the European savants about what these categories actually are—or how many there are—no one doubted that they would be the same the world over, independent of time (when one lived) or place. If "the primitives" seemed to think differently, then only because they were still closer to nature than to civilization—their capacity for reason had not yet fully emerged. Like children, they were caught in a state in which fiction and reality, reason and imagination had not yet differentiated themselves from one another.

Durkheim and Mauss took issue with this common wisdom. They agreed that the categories of the mind were the same the world over (in fact, they assumed that Aristotle's list of categories was accurate; Durkheim and Mauss 1902). However, they vehemently rejected the equation of the supposed primitives with children. The effort to explain the history of humanity in terms of the developmental psychology, their critique went, grounds in the assumption that humans at all times and in all places are freestanding individuals. And that, Durkheim and Mauss argued, is simply wrong. Humans don't live isolated lives onto their own. Instead humans live in society and are social beings: And how a human being thinks (about itself and the world) is ultimately inseparably related to the structure of the society to which that human being belongs (Durkheim 1912; see also Mauss 1931, [1938] 1950). If one wishes to understand why primitive people think differently, thus, there is no alternative to taking on a careful study of the structure of their societies.

What Durkheim and Mauss reported from their efforts to take on a sociological analysis of thinking, is that the more primitive a social structure is, the more primitive the thought processes of that society are. The example the two French anthropologists time and again relied on to prove their argument were the Aranda of Central Australia: if the Aranda seriously claimed that lizards or emus were their brothers, then this wasn't because they talked childish nonsense. On the contrary, it was because the Aranda—Durkheim and Mauss judged them to be the most primitive still living society—used their kinship system to order their natural surroundings. No surprise, then, that the plants and animals of their environment seemed to them part of their society.[28]

Gradually, over time—this was Durkheim and Mauss's rewriting of the eighteenth-century philosophies of history—as societies would get more differentiated, as different kinds of expertises would emerge, thought would differentiate itself as well. However, it would still—it would always—be contingent on the structure of society.

(The category of the individual, for example, was to them the distinctive product of our modern, highly differentiated and fragmented societies: an individual life, according to Durkheim and Mauss, was basically impossible in closely knit socities where no space for individual differences—let alone individualized life trajectories—existed.)

Lévy-Bruhl was troubled by the social ontology of Durkheim and Mauss. What triggered his hesitancy seems to have been his familiarity with German philosophy, to which the concept of society was entirely unknown. Indeed, it is a bit as if Lévy-Bruhl, an expert on German philosophical thought, wondered whether the concept of society, so central to French thought from Comte to Durkheim and Mauss, wasn't ultimately a French obsession rather than a breakthrough to the universal grounds of being human (as Durkheim and Mauss claimed).[29]

Was there any necessity to take for granted, as Durkheim and Mauss did, that all thought at all times was reducible to—and explicable by—the structure of the society in which one lived? Wasn't that a somewhat naïve exemption of "society" from the contingencies of history? Indeed, wasn't society itself a historical, and thus time-and-place-specific, category of thought?

Lévy-Bruhl felt provoked—and set out on his own explanatory journey: he began to read through ethnographic texts and soon began to argue that the categories of the mind were not at all universal. The philosophers—and Durkheim and Mauss—had gotten this completely wrong. He was convinced, and argued in many books and essays, that he had discovered that there was a general structure of *the* primitive mind as such, one that radically differed from the minds of the moderns: if the minds of the latter were logical, then the minds of the former were "pre-logical."

Lévy-Bruhl has been widely and wildly critiqued, for good reasons.

And yet his work opened up a possibility that excited ethnographers for much of the twentieth century: that elsewhere people might think in ways radically different from how Westerners think. Could that be?

A brief genealogy would have to hint at the work of Evans-Pritchard on the Azande and the Nuer (he exchanged letters with Lévy-Bruhl); Marcel Griaule and Germaine Dieterlen's research of Dogon thought; Meyer Fortes's exploration of the pattern of Tallensi sense making; Lévi-Strauss's juxtaposition of bricolage and engineering; Richard Horton's juxtaposition of African and European styles of thinking; or the rationality debate of the 1970s.[30]

the existential grounds of being human

The second conversation—or collaboration—of anthropologists with philosophers has, broadly speaking, concerned the exploration and (ethnographic) validation of the universal—existential—grounds of what it means to be human.

If the first conversation has a somewhat straightforward point of origin—Lévy-Bruhl's provocation of Durkheim and Mauss—that allows a somewhat linear genealogy, the second one is more dispersed and scattered: there are no clear starting points (or too many to be listed), and consequently there are no easily identified lines of descent. However, there is still a somewhat general pattern that one could describe thus: anthropologists read philosophical descriptions of the human condition (mostly of the late nineteenth and early twentieth century, mostly concerned with death, pain, suffering, disease, and angst as the horizon of the human) either to obtain a decoding tool that will allow them to make sense of the rituals of the people they study (with the effect that rituals mostly appear as societal organizations of existential passages), or to procure a language available for making faraway others visible—if under different cultural and social circumstances—as struggling with moral and existential questions familiar to their readers at home, with the consequence that a shared human space (a shared humanity experience) between the near ("us") and the far ("them") opens up.

It is a bit as if philosophers provided a theme—and anthropologists ethnographically documented its variation and thereby also its validity.

Even though the choice of philosophical authors is largely idiosyn-cratic—there are no schools of, say, Heideggerian anthropology—the list of philosophers of the human condition anthropologists have relied on is rather short. The most prominent are (in random order): Søren Kierke-gaard (specifically his reflection on being onto death and on angst and pain as markers of the human), Ludwig Wittgenstein (his ordinary lan-guage philosophy as much as his reflections on pain and the limits of lan-guage), William James (the variety of psychological experience), Martin Heidegger (on death and time, as well as on being thrown into the world), and, more recently, Emmanuel Levinas (his ethics of the other) and Gilles Deleuze (his concept of becoming).[31]

A recent edited volume by Das et al. (2014)—*The Ground Between: An-thropologists Engage Philosophy*—documents just how prominent this second form (still) is in contemporary anthropology.

departure

What difference does the departure from ethnos make? What is the effect of the dissociation of anthropology from ethnography on the relation be-tween anthropology and philosophy?

If one oversees the conversations between anthropologists and phi-losophers as they have taken place thus far, it appears that they have been organized by a rather one-sided division of labor, according to which phi-losophers provide the broader framework within which anthropology unfolds.[32]

Both exchanges, for example, the one on the primitive mind and the one on the universal existential grounds of the human, are—insofar as they are grounded in an interpretation of anthropology as ethnography (as the study of supposedly non-modern, mostly non-European societies)—contingent on the idea of a universal of history of humanity: they are con-tingent, that is, on the suggestion (1) that "humanity" comes in the form of a family of nations (societies); (2) that some of these societies (nations) are of an altogether different quality than European societies; and (3) that this difference—the difference between us and them—is ultimately a temporal difference.

All three—humanity, society, history—are arguably eighteenth- and nineteenth-century philosophical inventions that were unknown to prior times.

Anthropologists appear largely unaware of their contingency on philosophy. A quote from the introduction contributed by Arthur Kleinman, Michael Jackson, and Veena Das to *The Ground Between* provides a case in point—and also serves me to make clear the stakes of a departure from ethnos.

> We explicitly exclude from [our] consideration[s] the field of philosophical anthropology . . . since [for philosophers] anthropology was a term for reflections on the question of man rather than an empirical inquiry into the differences among human societies.[33]

Kleinman et al. write these lines as an explanation as much as a critique. Their reproach is that philosophers are merely concerned with "reflections" and the abstract ("man"), while anthropologists, experts of the real, are concerned with the "empirical" and the concrete ("human societies" as they actually exist).

Other anthropologists have made similar claims. For example, Didier Fassin, in the same volume, has claimed that the difference between anthropology and philosophy is that the former "makes sense of the world via scientific inquiry into a society."[34]

What Fassin and Kleinman and Das choose to forget (or are unaware of, it seems) is that their conception of anthropology—as the ethnographic study of society or of the differences among human societies—is actually itself the product of philosophical "reflection on the question of man." It is the product of a time-and-place-specific "philosophical anthropology" that was unknown prior to the eighteenth century (the concept of "society" and the suggestion that humans are "social beings"—beings who live in and are shaped by society—first emerged in the works of Montesquieu and Rousseau and was then later stabilized and ontologized by Adolphe Quetelet and Durkheim).

It thus is a bit as if the authors—whose works have opened up entirely new ways of anthropological research[35]—are unaware of the division of labor on which the concept of anthropology they uphold (anthropology as the ethnographic study of differences between human societies) is contingent: first the philosophers, experts of abstract reflections, work out a general theme, and then the anthropologists come along, self-declared experts of the concrete, and empirically document the ethnographic variation of the general theme worked out by philosophers.

They may understand their ethnographic reports as a critique of philosophy—of philosophers—and yet, their critiques remain contingent on the philosophical framework within which their critiques are articulated.

I think that just this ignorance (in the sense of not knowing) of one's contingency on philosophical concepts has been a distinctive feature of the vast majority of encounters between anthropologists and philosophers that occurred under the framework of classical modern ethnography.

The possibility of a philosophically inclined anthropology opens up in the very moment in which the framework philosophy has provided to anthropologists lose their evidence and become a problem: When (some) anthropologists find themselves compelled to abandon the study of "the differences among human societies" (call it ethnography) in favor of taking up "the question of man" *because the answers that philosophers had provided to this question—and that have organized anthropological research—have become visible in their historicity and contingency, with the consequence that anthropology has become an open question.*[36]

Once anthropology breaks free from ethnos (and its answer-based anthropology) and turns toward the human (question-based), it can bring its own condition of possibility, and hence its contingency on general philosophical setups, into a critical intellectual focus, making it into an explicit object of thought. What is more, it can expose its own conditions of possibility in its fieldwork/research and ask if today new ways of thinking and knowing the human are emerging, ways that escape the established philosophical concepts on which anthropology has thus far been contingent: humanity, the human, history, culture, society, the social, language, meaning subjectivity, and nature (all concepts the philosophy of modernity has assigned to it)?

Differently put: once anthropologists break with ethnos, anthropology has the potential to venture into the terrain it formerly left, unwittingly or not, to philosophy: a study of the conceptual grounds constitutive of the human and the real.

Anthropology itself can become philosophical.[37]

However, where philosophy has tended to provide conceptual grounds as a basis for universal knowledge production—or, at the very least, as formulations of general truths about the world / the human—the philosophically inclined anthropology (after ethnos) I try to bring into view here is interested in conceptual grounds only insofar as it wishes to get away from them. It puts them at stake in the concrete everyday scenes of fieldwork in order to let them get derailed, as a means to bring the new/different into view.

Not as a means towards an end (newer, better universal grounds) but rather as an end in itself (no more universal grounds).

One venue for an anthropology "after ethnos," thus, would be a philosophically inclined anthropology understood as the fieldwork-based study of thought—of concepts, of the categories that order thought at a given time in a given domain (international law, yeast biology, consulting, neuroscience, humanitarianism, film making, primatology, etc.), and of how these concepts and categories mutate over time (or mutate into new ones), thereby changing the order constitutive of things—among them the human thing—in ways for which no one has words or concepts yet.

Would it be a gross exaggeration to call it an empirical philosophy in its own right? And would it be a gross exaggeration to call this kind of empirical philosophy an ethical—virtuous—practice? Precisely insofar as in one's inquiry one exposes—puts at risk—one's ways of knowing and being?

What if anthropology were not conducted to produce knowledge or truth but as a philosophical exercise?[38]

Humans were not social beings prior to the eighteenth century?

They were not. Though note that the argument here is a conceptual one: perhaps humans have always lived in relations, in groups. However, these relations/groups were, prior to the late eighteenth century, not conceptualized as societies, and consequently humans could not be framed as social beings. The implication here is that the pattern of knowledge so familiar to us—society, the social, social context, social theory, social suffering—is not applicable to times that didn't know it, and that it might well be that today new spaces of living together open up that escape the logic of the social, thereby leaving the social sciences in jeopardy.[39]

philosophy/Philosophy

Philosophy? Are you serious? Why would you hold on to philosophy?

The question has followed and troubled me for some time. It is usually articulated as a mild—or straightforward—reproach: nineteenth century? Big old German men with beards? Dust? The primacy of reason and the pathos of the parochial?

I want to attempt an answer by opening up a distinction between "philosophy" and "Philosophy."

As a student in Germany, I was trained in capital-*P* Philosophy, as it revolves around *Vernunft* as expression of the *Geist*. I took classes on famous philosophers, mostly big men (many without beards, though), or on single books they have written. I learned to practice hermeneutics, that is, together with others I attended seminars in which we, under the guidance of professors (almost all men), worked meticulously through texts, slowly, one sentence, often one word, at a time. We reconstructed the thoughts an author articulated, deliberated why he used this and not that term and sought to reconstruct the conversations he had, the previous authors he reacted to, the development of his philosophy, and so on. In addition, I attended lectures in which exceptionally well-read Philosophy professors traced the subtle mutations of concepts through time, usually from the Greeks to the present, thereby making visible different epochs, each classified as different, somewhat clearly demarcated episodes in the history of reason (modernity might have been about fragmentation, but in its fragmentary quality it was still a fairly consistent epoch among epochs).

In many ways philosophy—lowercase *p*—is a whole different undertaking.

It is interested in thought, too—but in a different kind of thought, and in a radically different register. Lowercase-*p* philosophy does not attend to books (even if this sounds cliché) but to scenes of everyday life; it is not concerned with authors but rather with the presuppositions that are implicit, often in contradictory ways, in everyday life and that have no author.

I think of these presuppositions as *thought fragments*, or, alternatively, as nowhere clearly articulated *philosophies of life*.

I attend to these scenes—these philosophies (whether in the lab or in the market place). I collect them, arrange them, write their histories (how they appeared, how they changed over time), and annotate them as an effort to render visible the philosophies of life, of things, of relatedness, of the world they silently transport.

What interests me most, however, are instances in which the philosophies that have silently organized the everyday fail, in which something new/different occurs that escapes them and thereby breaks open a novel space that renders them useless, with the consequence that a radical uncertainty emerges where before there was nothing but taken-for-grantedness.

Not that I would be interested in the new "it" that might sooner or later emerge from such scenes—but because I am interested in the irreducible openness that reigns when no new "it" has yet emerged.

I call the practice of attending to the thought fragments that silently animate everyday life—this art of thinking about thought—philosophy.

At times I also call it poetry insofar as it attempts to capture that which cannot be captured. Or "political," in that it celebrates the impossibility of knowing or being known.[40]

Arguably there are resemblances with, echoes of, the millennia-old practice of thinking about thinking—of orienting oneself in thought, of transforming oneself into an object of thought to reach calmness of mind—described under the term "philosophy."[41]

But there are unbridgeable differences with the nineteenth- and the twentieth-century European practice of Philosophy.

Lowercase-*p* philosophy cannot afford—and couldn't think less about—the grandeur of capital-*P* Philosophy. It delimits itself with vehemence from the guardians of the Geist, whether they are tracing the history of reason, establishing the limits of what can reasonably be said, or simply regulate, by inventing rules, the use of words so that no accidents of thought might happen.

Lowercase-*p* philosophy isn't sovereign mastery (of what?). Instead it is a minor practice. It is the art of accidentally finding oneself in situations in which capital-*P* Philosophy—the presuppositions on which it has relied—are being dissolved. It doesn't give rise to (nor aspires to) the firm voice that articulates epochal ruptures, nor does it authorize truth claims—as truth is not what it is after. Instead it is interested in releasing things—the human—from truth.

thought/abstract, thought/concrete
(the problem with modernism)

"I wonder," a friend approached me after she had read an earlier version of chapter 1, "I mean just as a follow-up, what do you mean by 'thought'?"

"Are you uncomfortable," I asked back, a bit worried, "by my focus on thought?"

"Yes," she nodded. "I am. But in complicated ways."

"Can you explain?"

I knew from prior conversations—or presentations—that occasionally my talk about an anthropology of thought left people uncomfortable.

"Sometimes," she offered her critical reading, "you speak of thought as your own practice. Like you think or you orient yourself through thinking, thereby making something into an object of thought. I understand that and am with you. I think that thinking as a practice, or as a mode, as you call it, is really important. But at other times, and this is where I am really ambivalent, it sounds as if you suggest that thought itself, thought as such, exists. Is thought an actual object? Something that exists out there, in the abstract? A sphere unto itself?"

Thought in the abstract.

In a short text, published in 1900, just after he returned from his field expedition to the Torres Strait, W. H. R. Rivers had reported that his interlocutors, smart and skilled in so many ways, had proven themselves utterly incapable of abstract thought (1900:82): "The thought of people of the lower culture are highly developed so far as the concrete is concerned, while in abstract matters the terminology may be scanty and accompanied by a poor development of abstract thinking. The rule which follows is that the abstract should always be approached through the concrete."[42]

Ever since I first read these lines I have been fascinated by them. In my understanding, this is one of the very first instances where someone suggests that the possibility of getting at thought—the abstract—was to carefully immerse oneself into concrete, everyday life. What is more, it is one of the very first times someone suggested that life, as organized by thought, differs between people or societies.

To me, Rivers, together with Lévy-Bruhl (who, of course, was much less interested in fieldwork/the empirical), marked the beginning of the possibility of understanding anthropology as an empirical philosophy.

"Generally speaking," I replied, thinking of Rivers and Lévy-Bruhl, "I mean those vague presuppositions that somehow structure, in the form of background assumptions of which we mostly are not aware, what we do."

"And *you* can identify them?" my friend smiled, disconcertingly.

It took me some time to come to terms with this smile—and to learn to differentiate my first reply to her into two closely related and yet incommensurable ones.

reply 1

What do I mean by "thought"?

For the longest time, my reply would have been that I mean systems of thought: systems that underlie what we do, that silently organize our world and structure who we think we are, our sense of self.

My reference here is to a body of literature—one critical for my orientation—that ranges from anthropology (Rivers and Lévy-Bruhl, Evans-Pritchard, Durkheim, Mauss and Lévi-Strauss) to history (Bachelard and Canguilhem) and philosophy (Foucault).[43] Collectively, these authors have repeatedly suggested that there is an underlying grid—some call it a system, others speak of concepts or categories of thought, an episteme, a script—that is constitutive of things and of their relation with one another.[44]

Rivers, Lévy-Bruhl, Evans-Pritchard, Bachelard, Canguilhem, Foucault—I have not only spent years reading these authors. I have lived with and learned from them. I have loved them. And in some sense, I still do.

And yet, the smile of my friend led me to open up a difference.

Do I really want to suggest that behind the irreducible turbulences of everyday life there is a system? Am I really ready to suggest that the concrete is ultimately secondary to the abstract? Wouldn't this amount to upholding an unbearable "sovereignty of the abstract"? Wouldn't it imply a most awful, somewhat-nineteenth-century asymmetry between those who are capable of identifying the abstract—the really real—and those who are not?

The suggestion that there are people who are bound by the concrete and people who have access—who have broken through—to the abstract mirrors everything that is untenable about the self-understanding of one kind of modernism: while none of the authors I cite above is reducible to a technocracy of the abstract, there can be little doubt that there are echoes of just this technocracy in their works.

reply 2

What do I mean by "thought"?

My second reply emerges from a set of questions that were troubling me when I wrote up the first: Does the abstract actually exist? Are there really any underlying concepts, systems even, that one could identify as such?

My research led me to doubt that. As I see it, the abstract doesn't pre-date the concrete, on the contrary: the abstract is the product and hence the outcome of a study of the concrete. And all those who tend to the abstract as if it were the real thing, the actual condition of possibility—modernist technicians of the abstract, engineers of thinking—mistake as far as I can tell, the outcome of their research for a discrete object that had been silently waiting to be discovered.

This is not at all to say that there are no thoughts—or conditions of possibility—in everyday life. As a matter of fact, I conduct research to discover thoughts, to discover unarticulated presuppositions. Or to find myself in situations in which they become visible precisely because they no longer work.

However, I don't think that these thoughts exist independent of the very scenes in which they can be observed. What is more, at least in my experience, everyday life is almost always animated by more than one thought. Often by contradicting ones: life is ambiguous.

Call it the irreducible exuberance of everyday living.[45]

The challenge of the kind of anthropology I try to practice, thus, is to attend to the concrete and to stay, throughout, on the level of the concrete. It is this practice that I have in mind when I use the phrase "thinking about thinking/thought": it is a mode of orienting oneself, of relating to things, of gradually learning to transform them into an object of reflection—of thought—while simultaneously refusing the leap into the abstract.

From the perspective of the first answer, the concrete doesn't matter much. It is secondary, derived from the real thing, that is, the abstract. Consequently, the fieldworker, once she breaks through to the abstract, can discard the concrete. If she has any use of it at all, it is only as an illustration, that is, as an opportunity to render visible how the abstract organizes the concrete. From the perspective of the second answer, however, the illustration is all there is.

It is through the practice of thinking that one constitutes something as an object of thought, that one opens up the possibility of rendering visible the philosophical fragments that seem to organize the concrete (and that don't exist independent of the concrete, even if they are not reducible to the work of the anthropologist). In my most audacious hours I call this practice an art—the art of establishing relations with things, including the human thing, including oneself, in the genre of thought.

Can one render visible the fragments of thought that are implicit in everyday life—that seem to animate or organize it—without ever deserting into the abstract? Without ever leaving the terrain of the concrete? Can one arrange the concrete in such a way that the satisfaction to which the turn to the abstract aspires (but that it never achieves) arrives all by itself? Can one practice an anthropology of thought while rejecting the modernist sovereignty of the abstract? While, if in so many complicated ways, staying modern?
    I think so.

Of course, nothing of what I write here suggests that one shouldn't make abstractions. I certainly have indulged in the joy of abstraction many times.[46] However, it means to be careful not to mistake the abstract for the real thing (which would mean to forget that the abstract isn't any less concrete).[47]

escaping (the already thought and known)

I am afraid that there is a misunderstanding.

In the previous pages I occasionally suggested that one reason for conducting research is to escape "the established," "the already thought and known," "the taken for granted." Upon reflection, these formulations are somewhat unfortunate: they seem to convey the impression that one would already know, at the outset of one's research, what the taken for granted is. And that is wrong.

The taken for granted is an outcome of research, not its starting point. Indeed, one most powerful motivation for conducting fieldwork/research is precisely the wish to produce the already thought and known—in order to be able to escape it. Research (at least for some), means to put one's life on the line: it means to expose oneself, to hand oneself—one's concepts, one's way of being, one's way of orienting oneself—over to the unforeseeable chance events that make up fieldwork, hoping (waiting) to get derailed.

Fieldwork is a bit like the desire to find—or be found by—that which makes a difference; which cannot be subsumed without causing havoc; which suddenly or slowly makes visible our ways of thinking and doing as the merely taken for granted; which provokes a rupture, a rupture that produces an irreducible open (with the inevitable consequence that the taken for granted—or the open—is inseparably bound to/defined by the particular instance of the new/different one has accidentally become part of).

Differently put, the promise of research—its beauty—is the possibility that something one has thus far regarded as obvious—as so obvious that one could not possibly be aware of it—suddenly appears as problematic.

I add, first, that the fieldwork-based transformation of a given (one yet unknown at the outset of research) into an open question is hardly a linear process. I add as well, second, that fieldwork mostly doesn't generate unambiguous insights. The unforeseeable chance encounters fieldworkers tend to document in their notebooks, often don't add up in easy ways and often leave things in a state of uncertainty.

Is it an event? Has something new occurred? If yes, then in what sense? And to what degree?[48]

I add, furthermore, that it is precisely this uncertainty that the philosophically inclined anthropologist after ethnos is after: She celebrates the non-linear quality of her findings—because she is eager to render things, the world and the human as we knew it, ambivalent. She wants to detect and expose their uncertainty, their instability.

To the fieldwork-based anthropologist after ethnos, the mutation of certainty into ambivalence is a major outcome of her work.

Imagine the anthropology after ethnos, at least in its philosophically inclined variant, were a form of investigation—or better: an examination or exercise—that doesn't aspire to the production of truth but rather to the ceaseless generation of questions: a surplus of questions that no one could ever exhaust.

"of" the human

(after "the human")

ONE

What if anthropologists were to not just break with ethnos—with culture, society, territory—but with "the human" as well?

Can one conceive of an anthropology cut loose from "the human"? Can one imagine an anthropology decoupled from the figure of "Man" as it was consolidated in the second half of the eighteenth century and as it has since marked the condition of the possibility of anthropological research?[1]

What would such an anthropology after "the human" look like?

In what follows I struggle to provide a tentative answer—one among many possible answers—to this question. To be more precise, I attempt to provide a sketch of what one could call an anthropology *"of" the human / after "the human"*—a practice of fieldwork-based immersion that revolves around the discovery of the unanticipated: ways of thinking, possibilities of living that escape "the human," that cut through it, undermine it, dissolve it, render it useless.

Not as an end in itself but rather as a means to release humans—the world—from "the human."

How to come up with an anthropology that is anthropological *not* because it grounds its analysis in the already accumulated knowledge of the human—be it a variant of social theory or of cultural history—but because it brings into view instances that escape these groundings/accumulations?

The challenge is huge. At stake is not only a departure from culture and society, that is, with the presuppositions that humans are cultural and/or social beings. No, at stake is the radical abandoning of each one of the categories that have over the last 250 years stabilized "the human" from within.

The body, gender, the subject, suffering, experience, sex, emotions, nature, symbols, meaning, politics—each one of these concepts was first articulated in the context of the big eighteenth- and nineteenth-century project of finding human universals.[2] And each one of them silently transports a definite conception of "the human"—a normative, explanatory definition of what humans "are." Were one to ground one's research in any of these universals, one would inevitably foreclose the very possibility in which an anthropology "of" the human / after "the human" hinges: the possibility that unanticipated lines of thought, of being human, of living can emerge, possibilities that are incommensurable with "the human" (with the rather short list of existing definitions of the human that have made anthropology thus far possible).

Differently put, to begin one's analysis with universals would deny—make oneself blind to—the very cracks in the real on which the anthropology "of" the human (after "the human") is contingent.[3]

The challenge, thus, is to find ways to deanthropologize anthropology, to deanthropologize its concepts and methods. Not once and for all—but again and again. What if one were to understand anthropological research as the continuous, as the ceaseless deanthropologization of anthropology? A first step toward such a conception of anthropology, perhaps, is to write the history of—"the human."

———

But what could be more obvious than the fact that humans are "subjects" or that they have "a body"?

Yet neither of these concepts is obvious. The term "subject"—from the Latin *subiectum*, from the Greek *hypokaimenon*—emerged as an epistemological concept only in the seventeenth century and was meant to describe a human-specific (and -centric) way of seeing and experiencing and knowing the world (the line of flight emerges with Descartes and goes from there to Hume and Diderot and eventually to Kant).

The body is slightly younger. The idea that humans "are" a body, that their existence is grounded in a feeling, sensing, haptic, living universal organism that has a logic of its own, emerged only in the 1750s (in the writings of Georg Ernst Stahl, who coined the term "organism").[4] And it took another century—and the emergence of anatomy, surgery, and physiology—till the body was indeed established as a physiologically integrated, living organism and till the surgeon W. W. Keen could confidently tell his colleagues at the international surgery conference in 1897, "Surgery is the one and the same the world over. Whether in the frozen north or under the equator, in civilized America or barbaric Africa, be the patient white Caucasian, swarthy Negro, red Indian or yellow Malay, the same accidents and diseases assail him, the same remedies save him, identical operations cure him: a new remedy discovered in Japan is equally efficacious in Philadelphia; a new operation devised in America is equally applicable in Egypt."[5]

Could one expose the conceptual histories of these "human universals"—the subject and the body—in today's world and watch them get derailed?[6]

TWO

One of the earliest, still tentative formulations of "the human" appeared in an article that Denis Diderot (1713–1784) contributed in 1755 to the fifth volume of the *Encyclopédie, ou dictionnaire raisonnée des sciences, des arts, et des métiers*, which he edited, together with Jean le Rond d'Alembert (1717–1783), between 1751 and 1772.

"L'homme," Diderot writes in the article "Encyclopedia," "est le terme unique d'où il faut partir et auquel il faut tout ramener" (Diderot 1755).

The human is the unique term from which one has to begin and to which one has to return everything.

Diderot wrote his contribution to explain—and justify—why he and d'Alembert, together with the other members of their editorial collective, had organized their encyclopedia the way they did; it is as much a personal reflection as a justification of the massive project they embarked upon.[7]

It may seem, Diderot's explanation goes, that the obvious response to the question of how to best organize an encyclopedia is nature, that is, it should correspond to the natural order of things. However, he goes on, nature and its many objects would hardly be able to provide any sense of order at all. Nature is nothing but a long, confusing list of individual entries—we would face an infinite ocean of things, endless, boundless, never to be exhausted. Any sense of order that one would establish would be haunted by the arbitrary: "L'univers ne nous offre que des êtres particuliers, infinis en nombre, et sans presqu'aucune division fixe et déterminée; il n'y en a aucun qu'on puisse appeler ou le premier ou le dernier; tout s'y enchaîne et s'y succédé par des nuances insensibles."[8]

And anyhow, Diderot adds, nature by itself is boring and meaningless. What gives it meaning—what makes nature sublime and interesting—is "the human":

> Si l'on bannit l'homme ou l'être pensant et contemplateur de dessus la surface de la terre; ce spectacle pathétique et sublime de la nature n'est plus qu'une scène triste et muette. L'univers se tait; le silence et la nuit s'en emparent. Tout se change en une vaste solitude où les phénomènes inobservés se passent d'une manière obscure et sourde. C'est la présence de l'homme qui rend l'existence des êtres intéressante (. . .). Pourquoi n'introduirons-nous pas l'homme dans notre ouvrage, comme il est placé dans l'univers? Pourquoi n'en ferons-nous pas un centre commun? Est-il dans l'espace infini quelque point d'où nous puissions, avec plus d'avantage, faire partir les lignes immenses que nous nous proposons d'étendre à tous les autres points? Quelle vive et douce réaction n'en résultera-t-il pas des êtres vers l'homme, de l'homme vers les êtres? Voilà ce qui nous a déterminé à chercher dans les facultés principales de l'homme, la division générale à laquelle nous avons subordonné notre travail. . . . L'homme est le terme unique d'où il faut partir, et auquel il faut tout ramener.[9]

This is it, one of the very first programmatic formulations of an abstract, time-and-place-independent, in its ambition truly universal, category of "the human."[10]

According to Diderot, "the human" must not be thought of as a part of nature. For the human is effectively set apart from the sad and silent scene of nature as the contemplating, thoughtful being that is capable of producing what no other being can produce: meaning. Indeed, Diderot consistently argues in almost all of his writings that what distinguishes humans from all other beings, what is constitutive of their distinction, is their capacity to endow things with meaning.

In the mid-eighteenth century, the implications of Diderot's description of the human—of the conception of the human as it was upheld by the Encyclopédie—was as far-reaching as revolutionary (in the literal sense of the term): it suggested that whatever meaning one finds in the world, it is human made. And it implied that meaning, or the taken for granted, can be changed.[11]

If I referred to Diderot's formulation as still tentative, then it is because he granted the natural world a self-evident epistemological existence of its own. For Diderot and his contemporaries, the natural world was composed of discrete objects, each with its own properties and distinctions, properties and distinctions that (ever since René Descartes' 1636 *Discourse on Method*) everyone could see and know. Differently put, the natural objects, boring as they were, were epistemologically autonomous: they themselves, their properties, determined the knowledge humans could have of them.

A good thirty years after Diderot, Immanuel Kant's (1724–1804) *Kritik der reinen Vernunft* questioned just this epistemological autonomy (Kant 1781). In the preface to the second edition of his book in 1787 he wrote:

> Bisher nahm man an, alle unsere Erkenntnis müssen sich nach den Gegenständen richten; aber alle Versuch über sie a priori etwas durch Begriffe auszumachen, wodurch unsere Erkenntnis erweitert würde, gingen unter dieser Voraussetzung zunichte. Man versuche es daher einmal, ob wir nicht in den Aufgaben der Metaphysik damit besser fortkommen, dass wir annehmen, die Gegenstände müssen sich nach unserem Erkenntnis richten, welches so schon besser mit der verlangten Möglichkeit einer Erkenntnis derselben a priori zusammenstimmt, die über die Gegenstände, ehe sie uns gegeben werden, etwas festsetzen soll.[12]

Kant's argument is subtle. He wasn't a constructivist. His argument was not that all things are created by the human, that all things are, in their existence, contingent on the human. Instead the point he makes is that everything humans know is "constituted" by the a priori forms that, according to Kant, are the condition of the possibility of human knowledge.

To Kant human knowledge was reflective not so much of things in the world but rather of the specific form of which human knowledge was capable.[13]

What humans get to know, thus, was never a thing in itself—an absurd phrase for Kant—but a thing constituted by the formal a priori conditions of human knowledge. To understand these "transcendental" a priori forms of knowledge was the project he set for himself in his *Kritik der reinen Vernunft*.[14]

———

Note the subtle distinction between "creation" and "constitution," which escapes most of today's constructivists.

Kant thus went much further than Diderot: where the Frenchman merely suggested that all meaning was human made but still allowed for the objective, if boring, existence of natural objects to which humans could have unmediated access, Kant established the human as an universal epistemological—transcendental—principle that could never really reach beyond itself. With Kant the human itself became the condition of the possibility of whatever humans can know about the world, no matter where and when they lived.

The consequence of Kant's philosophy was that the only thing humans could ultimately be concerned with was—epistemologically speaking—in the last instance, the human itself. Kant was quite aware of this consequence and formulated it himself when he explained that, today, all of philosophy had become reducible to one question only: "What is the human?"[15]

THREE

Around the turn from the eighteenth to the nineteenth century, Kant's reconfiguration of the human (which had built on and departed from Hume who, in turn, had built on and departed from Descartes) gave rise to the massive decoding project of the human sciences in general and of anthropology in particular.

First came the learned societies (the Société des observateurs de l'homme was founded in 1799); then the philosophical-anthropological (Feuerbach and Nietzsche) and political-anthropological (Marx and Engels) critique; and eventually the new discipline called anthropology (the first museums and chairs of anthropology were created only in the 1870s).

While obviously many things have changed since the first, still fragile emergence of the human sciences in the early nineteenth century, it seems hardly an exaggeration to say that "the human" still, to this day, marks the condition of the possibility of the human sciences in general and of anthropology in particular. Anthropology was invented as, and in many respects still is, the science of human reality—a reality defined in its scope by an abstract, in its aspirations universal (time and place independent) conception that first emerged in Europe in the second half of the eighteenth century.[16]

Without the emergence of "the human," there would be no anthropology, neither past nor present.

———

With just a little effort one could draw a line, multiply broken and yet recognizable, from the late eighteenth century to contemporary American anthropology. First, there is the line from Kant, careful reader of Rousseau, to Herder (1744–1803), who had taken classes with Kant in Königsberg in the 1760s and who had formulated, in the 1780s, the project of a cultural history that was constitutive of German anthropology. From Herder the line continues to Adolf Bastian (1826–1905). Bastian had been among those few who institutionalized Herder's anthropology in German universities. He was founding director of the Berlin Anthropological Museum and cofounded the Berlin Society for Anthropology. And he was perhaps the first to take up Herder's challenge empirically: Bastian traveled the world for over thirty years and wrote over eighty books. Next the line runs to Franz Boas (1858–1942), who had been a student of Bastian's in Berlin in the 1880s and who famously founded American cultural anthropology as a spin-off of Herder's cultural history. Indeed, some of Boas's early American texts read like English renderings of Herder, specifically of his *Auch eine Geschichte der Menschheit* (Herder 1774). From Boas, finally, the line leads, via his many students (most notably Ruth Benedict and Margaret Mead) to Clifford Geertz (1926–2006) or Marshall Sahlins (1930–)—and from there to the present.

What follows from this brief history of "the human" is that the general, abstract concept of "the human," understood as a category under which all humans of all times and places could be subsumed as if they were members of a single collective—"humanity"—can hardly be taken for granted. "The human"—just as well as the category of "humanity"—is not a universal, a timeless ontological category that has always existed. Instead it is a recently invented concept that emerged in Europe about 250 years ago and that became subsequently universalized.

Could one interpret this recentness of "the human" as an invitation for research? Could one, for example, ask if there are, today, in the here and now, instances that are such that they logically—conceptually—escape (or exceed) the concept of "the human" as it emerged in the eighteenth century? Instances that release the human from "the human"? Could one meticulously map the new, unanticipated venues for being human—for living a life—they are opening up?[17]

It is from these questions that the possibility of an anthropology "of" the human / after "the human" emerges.[18]

FOUR

If I stress here the contingency of anthropology on the emergence of "the human" that is because it is precisely this contingency that gives contour to the challenge of formulating an anthropology "of" the human / after "the human."

How to depart from "the human"—celebrating the irreducible openness, the uncertainty, that emerges from this departure—without foreclosing the very possibility of, well, anthropology?[19] How to practice an anthropology after "the human" without immediately succumbing to what one could call a mere replacement approach? That is, the substitution of "the human" by another—supposedly better, in the sense of truer—epistemological foundation (the replacement of one form of closure/fundament, say culture, by another form of closure/fundament, say material semiotics—or ANT [Actor-Network Theory] or radical alterity)?[20]

———

Can one practice anthropology as the ceaseless effort of deanthropologizing anthropology (and not just anthropology)?

———

The answer I want to try out here—think of it as an experiment—is what one could call *an analysis of movement / in terms of movement*.

At stake in this experiment—in this kind of analysis—is the possibility of a study of conceptual mutations that is itself not grounded in an unmoved analytical Archimedean point that is external to the movement one studies (the human, dialectics, enunciation, ANT, nature-cultures, performativity, affect, *homini sacri*, and many other candidates).

Put in a formula, the idea is to render visible ruptures and mutations of established conceptions of the human (*an analysis of movement*) by way of bringing into view how instances in the here and now derail and defy the normative conceptions of the human (or other things, really) that are silently transported by the analytical concepts on which anthropology thus far has relied (*in terms of movement*).

The form such an analysis of movement / in terms of movement would take is what I refer to as *exposure*: the exposure of oneself, of one's analytical categories, of the established conceptions of the human that are built into these categories, in one's fieldwork/research. The task would consist in immersing oneself into scenes of everyday life in order to let the chance events that make up fieldwork/research give rise to an unanticipated, unforeseen difference.

What I mean by "difference" is an observation—a recognition, a discovery, a surprise that suddenly or slowly mutates a given into a question, that makes visible something one simply took for granted as contingent on a recent conceptual history.

What is more, I mean a discovery of a space/a realm, the dynamic of which—its speed, its velocity, its logic of composition—is no longer reducible to this conceptual history, that escapes it.

The challenge of this type of research, then, would be to use unanticipated fieldwork-based derailments of one's analytical vocabulary—of the conception of the human this vocabulary transports—to bring into view that (and how) instances in the present outgrow the conceptual histories that have until now stabilized it. The challenge would be to bring into view singular openings and to understand them as an invitation to reinvent, just for the sake of one's project, the very condition of the possibility of anthropology (while avoiding the mistake of presenting this new/other anthropology as the one and only breakthrough to the real; this would be a replacement approach).

Were one to conduct such an analysis of movement / in terms of movement, one would study the human, after "the human."

FIVE

The effects of the letting go of "the human" on research are most far-reaching—and at first overwhelming, almost deleterious. Once cut loose from the epistemic figure that until recently defined what anthropology is and can be about, anthropologists are free to venture into the world and to stray away—far-away—from human affairs and world making.

The explosion in scope is enormous—and exhilarating.

———

It is not that the anthropologist after "the human" wouldn't care about humans. At stake is no anti-humanism (and one could anyhow argue that one powerful form of attending to humans is to turn away from them). No, the background to the departure from a focus on people, rather, is the methodological refusal to ground one's analysis in the epistemological grounding principle the human has been ever since Kant.[21]

———

But what then does an anthropologist "of" the human study?

She studies how human and non-human instances—or entanglements of both—exceed the categories that have grounded anthropology (the human sciences) thus far. She studies the emergence of concepts, the ways in which their emergence has reconfigured the real, the ways in which they have mutated over time. And she studies the here and now, curious to find instances that expose and derail the concepts that have not even been noticed as — concepts.[22]

Take, for example, something as (traditionally) far away from the human as bacteria. Such an anthropology of bacteria can take a multitude of forms; it can map the emergence of conceptual and experimental reconfigurations of bacteriology since the late nineteenth century (and show that the concept "bacteria" never was fully stabilized); it can show how bacteria effectively have produced and continue to produce the world, from their steady production of oxygen to their critical role in the nitrogen cycle to the absorption of CO_2: it can render visible and available the beauty of biogeochemistry; it can show the dependency of our hearts and our brains on microbial metabolites produced in our guts; it can insert, or expose, the human in the epistemic space(s) produced by bacteria and see if it gets derailed (and if so, how).[23]

Or it can tell the story of the gingko tree, hundreds of millions of years old; it can tell the story of its habitats, of its art of reproduction, of its many migrations, of its near extinction about 100,000 years ago, and of its grandiose reemergence over the last two hundred years, when only a few trees were left: gingko, too, produces the world, it gives it a distinctive temporality and structure — a structure from the perspective of which humans are a side note at best.[24]

What would it take to learn to think about humans from the perspective of the gingko? What concepts would one have to devise to achieve this? What understandings of the world / of humans would an anthropology of gingkoes allow for? Or an anthropology of wave patterns in the Pacific Ocean, of matsutake, of frozen methane bubbles in the Greenland ice sheet, of cheese, of Ebola, of snails, of Hurricane Katrina, of the neoliberal social, L1 jumping genes, or of SpaceX?[25]

———

Would it be much of a provocation if one were to say that what becomes visible once "the human" has lost its evidence is what one could call the stunning conceptual poverty that has characterized anthropology throughout its roughly 250-year-old history?

It is against this background of impoverishment that I celebrate what one could call the inexhaustible conceptual richness of the anthropology "of" the human / after "the human."[26]

In closing I want to prevent two misunderstandings.

First, the effort to work out a possibility for an anthropology after "the human" doesn't imply that anyone "still" interested in things human is a hopeless relict of a past long gone. Rather, it is meant as an invitation to wonder, among other things, about how to bring into view things human without relying on the anthropological vocabularies that have silently organized thinking about humans and human life.[27]

Second, the anthropology "of" the human doesn't let go of the human in order to replace it with a better in the sense of truer or morally superior account of the world (the candidates are many, running from ANT to mushrooms and from forests to insects). For the anthropologist "of" the human such a "replacement approach" would ultimately amount to little more than a substitution of one kind of closure by another, where the challenge would be to maintain the open, to allow it to flourish. The irreducible openness provoked by the break with "the human"—when the real is released from the already thought and known—would be immediately exhausted by a new set of normative (foundational) claims.[28]

An anthropology "of" the human / after "the human" is quite literally, has quite literally to be, *research into the open.*

———

It needs to be said: the open doesn't exist. There is no open *as such*, a single, identical, in the sense of unchanging, ontological open that would stand behind all conceptually constituted reality, that one could know and then identify again and again. What I refer to as open is simply the nonteleological movement that reigns when an established form of knowing—of organizing—is undermined while no new one has yet emerged that would give it direction (a telos). The particular quality—form (if this is the right word at all)—of such a nonteleological movement is in each instance singular, depending on the formation that has been undermined, on the event that broke it open, on too many things to be mentioned here. It is in each instance singular, incomparable.

cataloguing

"How is your work different from the work of Paul Rabinow or Ian Hacking?"

The question was raised after I had presented a much earlier version of the previous chapter.

"Can you say more?" I asked back. "I think it would help me if I understood where you see parallels."

"Well," my listeners responded, "you said that you are interested in the human, in the emergence of new ways of thinking the human. And it seems to me as if this is exactly what the work of Hacking or Rabinow is about."

I found the question remarkable. After all, it is by no means evident that someone would recognize that Hacking's "making up people" and Rabinow's "anthropos + logos" are related projects.

"This is a great summary of the work of Hacking and Rabinow," I replied. "But can you tell me why you think that my work is a version of theirs?"

It felt a bit odd to return the question yet again, but then, over the years I had learned that one way to respond to a question that one doesn't fully understand and for which one has no good answer yet is to politely but persistently ask back, until one understands where the question is coming from.

"Well," the young man replied with impatience, "you seem to just map new ways of making up humans. And that was the innovation of Hacking and Rabinow. So is there any difference?"

"Now I see," I said. "You think that I map, with Rabinow's words, the emergence of new logoi of anthropos, or, with Hacking's words, how people make up people. You are absolutely right that I owe much to these thinkers. They were my teachers, and it was through their works that I learned to recognize a certain line that revolves around thought, about how it changes over time in often unanticipated, discontinuous ways. I also learned from them to relate such mutations to the human. They have both arguably shaped my thinking, as has my colleague Allan Young, who also should be mentioned here."[29]

I tried to move to the next question, but the listener intervened.

"Would you mind explaining where your work differs from these white men, if at all?"

The whole room laughed.

"Oh well," I began, "I had hoped I could trick you. See, it is odd for me to reply to your very intelligent questions. Everything I say is going to be held against me. But the long and the short of it is that I think that I have begun moving in another direction. I have no critique to offer. It is just that I think that over the last few years I have been interested in questions and possibilities that exceed the work of Hacking and Rabinow or, better, that cannot be addressed with the vocabulary they invented to address the problems that concerned them. Different problems, different conceptual challenges."

Curiously, I looked at the young man who had insisted I reply.

"It is very difficult to make you give a concrete answer," he replied.

Again the whole room laughed.

"Oh," the tape records me saying, not without a notion of self-defense, "but maybe I have no good answer. Or maybe I don't want to have one because I don't want to be critical of authors I admire. But if you insist, I think what I've learned over the last couple of years, partly from my research, partly from reading works that explore the possibility of an anthropology of the natural, nonhuman world, partly from conversations with friends, partly from reading and rereading Foucault again and again, and partly from my nascent research in AI, has been that the generation of anthropologists and philosophers who have learned from Foucault have, implicitly or explicitly, preserved a version of nineteenth-century humanism. What I mean by this is that in their works they never exceed—nor did they try to exceed—the frame that the emergence of 'the human' has established."

"How so?" the woman who had invited me to present my work now asked, obviously provoked by my reply.

"I knew I should not have gotten into this," I replied with a sigh. "I think that Hacking's work evolves around two related but separate themes, the emergence of new styles of reasoning, and the way such new styles of reasoning make up people. More specifically, Hacking is interested in how the emergence of new ways of 'labeling people'—of classifying them according to new categories—results in people using these categories to think of themselves (and/or of other people). The provocation of this approach is that some of the categories we have taken for granted today come into view as of rather recent origin. The project that emerges from this provocation is a history of the many different ways in which people could, over the course of time, think of themselves. Fair?"

My host nodded, as did most people in the audience.

"Where Hacking measures conceptual mutations with the ruler of reason, Rabinow works from amidst fieldwork scenes. But his question is related to Hacking's. In *Anthropos Today*, for example, one can read that 'naming and analyzing the form of anthropos is the logos of one kind of anthropology. How to best think about the arbitrariness, contingency, and powerful effects of those forms constitutes the challenge of that type of anthropology.' I think this overlap between Hacking and Rabinow is partly due to the fact that they both worked closely with Foucault. Also fair?"

Again my listeners nodded.

"Well, so I think that Hacking and Rabinow both stay within what one could call 'the human framework.' Who makes up people? Who creates new labels? The answer is people. And who creates, accidentally or not, new logoi of anthropos? Again, the answer is people (or assemblages made by people). So behind the change Hacking and Rabinow allow for, radical change to be sure, there is a somewhat unchanging anthropology according to which people make up people.[30] So if you ask me for a difference, then I say that ultimately, were one to follow the lead of Hacking and Rabinow, one's work would eventually assume the form of a catalogue. One would catalogue ways in which people make up people. Certainly such a catalogue would be extraordinary. It would be rich and curious, full of perplexing discoveries and observations. But it would also be a study of movement that doesn't move. After all, behind every single change stands—the human."

"So all the two can map are variations of the already known: they constantly reproduce the world we are already familiar with," the young man replied.

"This sounds too critical, as if they made a mistake. They didn't make a mistake. Rather, Hacking and Rabinow addressed a different set of questions. One more neutral way of articulating the challenge would be to say, imagine a Cartesian system, the x-axis of which is nature, and the y-axis of which is culture. Most of the human sciences allow for the continuous appearance of new dots within this fixed Cartesian system. They are enthralled by the inexplicable curves they discover, and celebrate diversity. And that is wonderful. So what happened is that I noted, and this is not very spectacular, that they always exempt the x-axis and the y-axis from all change. At first I wasn't quite sure what to do with this observation. I found it very delimiting, but I also didn't know how to break free. Gradually, then, the idea emerged that one way to get rid of these limitations is to expose the condition of possibility of one's own work in one's research, so that it can get derailed. One would need to put the whole Cartesian system as such at stake and see if it gets derailed. Wouldn't that be very interesting? And I think that such derailments of 'the human' can occur in the human realm, as the seminal work of Stephen Collier or Jim Ferguson clearly shows. They both have mapped how the neoliberal social exceeds and undermines the "social" of the social sciences. And they have both taken up the challenge of rethinking, on the one hand, where the "social" of the social sciences came from, and, on the other, what a critical science that neither can nor wants to rely on the "social" of the social sciences anymore could look like. But such derailments can occur as well in the nonhuman, natural realm, which the work of Stefan Helmreich, Hugh Raffles, Nicolas Langlitz, Heather Paxson, or Anna Tsing shows."

"These authors," he suggested, "allow the real to exceed their concepts, to liberate their analysis from the constraints that one's concepts inevitably are."

"Well, I would add that what you call constraints are only constraints given the particular kind of curiosity that these authors have found themselves confronted with. They cannot be constraints as such. If they were, then one would have broken through to a general truth. What I am interested in, though, is to get away from such breakthrough stories."[31]

antihumanism

I am hardly the first to ask how one could liberate the human sciences from the human. Louis Althusser (1918–1990) and Michel Foucault (1926–1984) asked this question fifty years before I did. However, there are major differences between the projects of the two French intellectuals and the project I try to bring into view here. And one of these differences is particularly instructive.[32]

When Althusser coined the term "antihumanism" in his essay "Marxism and Humanism" (1965), his aim was to trouble what was then a popular trend in French philosophy: the fusion of humanism and Marxism. To Althusser, the very idea that Marxism could be understood as a form of humanism was an intolerable betrayal of the critical insights of Marx. It is true, Althusser concedes, that the young Marx thought of himself as a humanist. But around 1845, he goes on, Marx made what was one of his most critical and far-reaching "discoveries":[33] that "the human" was a product of the bourgeoisie. The consequence of Marx's discovery was that the assumption that history is made by humans, even if they don't know it (because of their alienation from human nature), had become as untenable as the suggestion that the goal must be to return history to humans.[34]

Althusser's ambition was to abstract a general warning from what he calls "Marx's theoretical anti-humanism": what his contemporaries had to understand was that any form of humanism is ultimately a representation of the understanding of the human of the dominant class of a society and hence must be rejected as idealism.

Any grounding of history in the human was a mistake.

But how, then, to understand history? Althusser points to historical materialism, which he describes as Marx's reply to his earlier humanism. The advantage of historical materialism was that it allowed for an analytical comprehension of history that relies not on the human but on historical modes of production, which exceed the human, which produce different conceptions of the human.[35]

This was Althusser's problem/ambition: to come up with a philosophy of history that was not grounded in "the human."

Foucault described his own departure from the human as "the hard work of freedom" (1972, 13). In his Les mots et les choses ([1966] 1990) he had shown just how recent the concept of "the human" was—and in its aftermath he found himself confronted with a challenge that was reminiscent of Althusser: how could one write history without relying on the eighteenth-century concept of "the human"?

Although Althusser had the comfort of relying on the authority of Marx, Foucault was as wary of Marxism as he was of humanism or, for that matter, all teleologies and transcendentals. The challenge he thus faced—and that he addressed in his *L'archéologie du savoir* (1969)—was somewhat more encompassing: Foucault had to come up with a whole new theory of history, of what it was and of how it could be analyzed.[36]

Foucault's solution was discourse analysis. Where the bourgeois historians understood history as grounded in a continuum—behind every event in time stands what he condescendingly called "the subject"—Foucault suggested to instead analyze "the structures of speech" that organize "discursive enunciations" of whole periods of time and that exceed the humans "who make these enunciations."[37]

Take all the documents written in a randomly defined period, he suggested, and anonymize them, so that you have one giant single text, a text with many origins that stretches out over centuries. Then analyze the structures that organize this single text, work out the grammar that silently informs it (a grammar that, as it stretches across centuries and many authors, can never be reduced to any human subject or intentionality). More specifically, analyze if this grammar—which according to Foucault is constitutive of reality—at one point changes, if it undergoes a sudden unanticipated rupture that allows one to clearly demarcate a before and an after.

Can you find any such "radical ruptures" (Foucault 1972, 5)?[38]

Foucault's ambition was not only to work toward a new understanding of history. He also hoped to provide new foundations—a new set of dehumanized (desubjectified) analytical categories that would replace the humanistic categories and that could serve, from now on, to produce knowledge "freed from the anthropological theme": discourse, series, limit, thresholds, strategy, ruptures, displacement, enunciation, transformations. Indeed, *The Archeology of Knowledge* was Foucault's new "general theory" of history.[39]

Arguably, this effort to ground a historical analysis in analytical vocabulary free from "the human" (or "the subject") continued to be a critical feature of Foucault's thought when, in the 1970s, he introduced the concept of a *dispositif* (in English often rendered as "apparatus") as a kind of reaction to the somewhat exclusive focus on abstract epistemic structures of his earlier work (Foucault 1980).

From the perspective of the kind of anthropology I try to bring into view here—an anthropology interested in how instances in the here and now escape the human and open up previously unknown possibilities of thought—the work of Althusser and Foucault (the Foucault of the late 1960s / early 1970s) is as intriguing as it is unfortunate. It is intriguing in that their works effectively provincialize and problematize "the human"; it is unfortunate in that the form taken by their radical rupture with the "anthropological theme" (Foucault [1969] 1972, 17) was ultimately the effort to come up with new foundations that aspired to be as constitutive as the "transcendental human" had been (in Althusser's case historical materialism, in Foucault's discourse analysis).

One could speak of a replacement approach, insofar as both Althusser and Foucault replaced one closed form with another closed form.

If I called the work of Althusser and Foucault instructive, then it is precisely because their replacement approach brings into sharp focus the challenge one faces when one sets out to elaborate the possibility of an anthropology "of" the human / after "the human": the one thing it cannot afford is to close the openness that emerges when one releases the human—and anthropology—from "the human." It cannot because it is exactly this openness that provides the condition of possibility on which its existence is contingent: the possibility that new yet unknown and unanticipated spaces of thought break open that exceed and thereby undermine the established ways of thinking and knowing.[40]

An anthropology "of" the human / after "the human" is not only quite literally *research into the open*; it is also an attempt to render visible and available the beauty of the open.

a disregard for theory

One powerful implication of an anthropology "of" the human / after "the human" is a certain disregard—disrespect—for theory. By "theory" I mean the postulation of an explanatory scheme (usually in the form of a first principle) that is used to decode a particular phenomenon in general, world-explaining terms. It is a causal, coherently worked out hypothesis that offers explanations (a truth about the world).[41]

The reason for this disregard for theory is the observation that theories deny the possibility of the openness constitutive of the anthropology "of" the human: the recognition that the new/different is conceptually incommensurable with the already thought and known. Theories already know (everything). A theorist—that is, someone who theorizes a particular instance in order to explain—has to assume that, of course, she has the key to understanding the world. How else would the act of decoding that a theory offers—say in terms of social class or in terms of performance theory—be plausible?

But what if the thing one attempts to think through in terms of this or that theory, in its own dynamic, in its own singular conceptual configuration, were such that it actually defies the theory used to explain it?

Let's take social theory.

What is so profoundly delimiting about social theory, if only from the perspective of the openness that is constitutive of the anthropology "of" the human, is that whatever phenomenon a social theorist will investigate—it will be framed as "social." Wherever one turns, all one finds is social struggle, social injustice, social suffering, the reproduction of social asymmetry, and so on.

I am aware that such a formulation is provocative. However, my aim here is not to deny struggle, injustice, suffering, asymmetry. Rather, my aim is to point out that by labeling each one of these phenomena as social, one transports a closed definition of the human (as social, as living in society) that literally locks the human (the world) into a particular epistemological scheme that is as contingent as the things it is supposed to explain.

What if one were to focus one's attention not only on struggles, injustices, suffering, asymmetries—but also on the question of whether the instances one studies are such that they escape the logic of the social as it first emerged somewhere between Adolphe Quételet (1827, 1835, 1848) and Émile Durkheim (1893, 1895, 1897) in the late nineteenth and early twentieth century, a logic that remains constitutive of most social theory? What if one were to take the social not as a breakthrough to the universal but as a provincial configuration of the human (of the real)? The implication would be that there might well be many instances that, in their own conceptual configuration and dynamic escape the constitution of the real (the human) as social. Just as well one could ask how one's discoveries escape the efforts by DeLanda (2006) or Latour (2005) to come up with new, and from their perspective better (in the sense of truer), conceptions of the social.

It is not that social theory would not be useful or interesting. What makes social theory—or any theory, really—into a problem, rather, is that it mistakes the provincial for the universal; that it reduces the yet unknown to a particular, provincial conception of things human (after all, it will be social); and that it denies the very possibility that things could be different (that new ways of thinking, knowing, and existing could emerge).

The consequence, from the perspective of what one could call an anthropology of the open, is boredom in the face of the eternal repetition of a script—society.

Expressed in more general terms, built into theory (whether social or cultural or otherwise) is a kind of closure. A closure that denies the undefined openness that is constitutive of the anthropology "of" the human; it denies the possibility that things could be otherwise than they are (or seem); that mutations of the possible might occur that we cannot grasp with our already established ways of thinking and knowing.

It is a bit as if theory were a prison, designed to prevent "the hard work of freedom" (Foucault 1972).

Theories aspire to be timeless, whereas the philosophically inclined anthropology "of" the human is interested in precisely the timeliness of things (or how a given instance escapes the concept of timeliness). Theories are interested in the general and seek to describe the specific in general terms, whereas the kind of anthropology I try to bring into view here is interested in precisely those aspects of the present that cannot be subsumed under the general. Theories provide causal schemas—first principles such as society or culture—whereas the anthropologist of emergent ways of thinking is interested in developments that escape these first principles, that set them in motion, that undermine them, that lead to new yet unexplored ways of explaining (which only the narrow-minded would want to ontologize). Theories determine analytical attentions (or sensibilities), whereas an anthropologist "of" the human attempts to find out if new forms of attention / new kinds of sensibilities are coming into existence.[42]

Theories might be good to think with; they may be fascinating, stimulating, eye-opening—something one has to know. And yet, the possibility of the anthropology "of" the human is, precisely insofar as it is research-oriented, informed by a profound disregard for—theory. When the task is to report on the emergent/different, when the goal is to document and capture the dynamic caused by singular events that escape the already established and thereby introduce motion in a field of knowledge, theory is hardly useful.

Sure enough someone is going to read this and argue that what I present here is just another theory. But is it? I don't think so. The purpose of these lines is to make *escape* a central aspect of research, that is, an instance that escapes the already thought and known and thus allows for an unanticipated openness that ridicules any theory. With Félix Guattari and Gilles Deleuze (1994, 5), one could say that the aim of an anthropology "of" the human / after "the human"—of an analysis of movement / in terms of movement—is to capture the "always new."

Could one make a distinction between "theory" and the "theoretical"?

no ontology

Over the last ten years, since roughly the early 2000s, something quite extraordinary has happened in the human sciences. An unprecedented, unanticipated event has taken place: anthropologists have gradually expanded their inquiries to the nonhuman, natural world.

It is difficult to provide an explanation for this expansion.[43] In retrospect it may seem as if the possibility for an anthropology of the natural world was brought about by the early works of Donna Haraway and Bruno Latour.[44] But upon closer examination, this is hardly the case. Haraway's *Primate Visions* or Latour's *We Have Never Been Modern*, for example, were written and read, respectively, as political and philosophical critiques of the nature/culture distinction—not as calls for an actual anthropology of insects (Raffles 2011) or mushrooms (Tsing 2015).

It thus seems as if a new, in many ways unanticipated, venue of research emerged in the early 2000s. A genealogy of this emergence would have to gesture to Michael Pollan's *The Botany of Desire* (2001), which was arguably one of the first attempts to think about humans from the perspective of plants and bumblebees; to Donna Haraway's *The Companion Species Manifesto* (2003)—which indeed was so new and different at the time (an event) that when it was first published few people knew how to read it—and her *When Species Meet* (2008); Stefan Helmreich's *Alien Ocean* (2009); Hugh Raffle's *Insectopedia* (2011); Heather Paxson's *The Life of Cheese* (2012); Anna Tsing's *The Mushroom at the End of the World* (2015); Kath Weston's *Animate Planet* (2017); it would also have to refer to the official presentation, in cultural anthropology, of a new subdiscipline called "multispecies anthropology" (Kirksey and Helmreich 2010; see as well Kirksey 2014a, 2014b). And it would have to mention that around 2012, amid the critique and excitement provoked by the study of multispecies encounters, a line of research constituted itself that has become known over the last few years as ontology. The reference here is, on the one hand, to work coming out of science and technology studies (STS), most famously Annemarie Mol (2002), with Bruno Latour and John Law in the background, and, on the other hand, to a line of more classical modern ethnography that emerged from work in the Amazon. Here the reference is mostly (but not exclusively) to Eduardo Viveiros de Castro (2014), Philippe Descola (2013), and Eduardo Kohn (2007).

Among anthropologists, this coming together of an anthropology of nonhuman species or of multispecies encounters (both of which are very much after ethnos) and classical modern ethnography under the rubric of ontology has received a lot of attention (on blogs as well as in journals). It has even been argued that anthropology is undergoing an "ontological turn," which is changing what anthropology is about and how it is practiced (Holbraad 2009; Paleček and Risjord 2013; Holbraad et al. 2014; Reyes 2014; Kohn 2015).

As ontology seems to partly revolve around an effort to break with "the human," and thus around the topic of the previous chapter, it seems prudent to indicate that the project I have sought to outline moves in a direction radically different from the project of the ontologists, and why this is so. I offer six observations.

OBSERVATION 1

My first observation introduces a distinction. In my reading, anthropologies of nonhuman species or of multispecies encounters and ontology are two somewhat different projects. I am not saying there is no overlap (see Kirksey 2012, 2014), but where many multispecies anthropologists focus on what one could call the anthropological effects of a given nonhuman species (of how they put human exceptionalism in question) or on the encounters of different species (and the new possibilities for thinking about living together that such encounters open up), the ontologists are busy articulating a new general theory of the real as such, of its actual ontological structure.

While many of the multispecies authors are interested in undermining the nature/culture distinction that has stabilized the anthropological exceptionalism on which anthropology has largely been based, ontologists are interested in correcting an error: their ambition is to replace the mistake of the moderns with a theory adequate to how the world actually "is" (hence, ontology). Somewhat inevitably, then, the ontologists are celebrating their work as a breakthrough to the truth (a breakthrough often presented as a moral remedy). Such a celebration is absent from (most) multispecies anthropology; it doesn't need it.[45]

Why "ontology"?

In an essay on the history of the idea that knowledge has a history, Georges Canguilhem (1966) argues that the term "epistemology" was coined in 1854, by James F. Ferrier, to mark a departure from ontology. In the early nineteenth century, Canguilhem writes, it had increasingly become clear that the knowledge produced by the sciences radically escaped the ontologies philosophers had worked out over the previous centuries. A first and somewhat immediate effect of this escape was that the taken-for-granted world—the natural cosmos of which humans were a part—collapsed (Canguilhem locates this event in the second half of the eighteenth century). A second effect became evident only gradually, when the steady emergence of new knowledge (especially in physics) time and again rendered established knowledge obsolete: the recognition that all knowledge about the world is methodologically mediated and grounded in conceptual presuppositions that are potentially undermined by new discoveries. According to Canguilhem, Ferrier introduced the term "epistemology," then, precisely to bring into view this conceptual instability of scientific knowledge.

In the middle of the nineteenth century knowledge began to have a history—insofar as it was recognized as being contingent on (if not reducible to) humans (for a similar argument, see Rheinberger 2010).

Canguilhem's observations are instructive insofar as the opposition between ontology (a somewhat closed natural cosmos) and epistemology (the breaking open of this cosmos) is a recurrent theme in the writings of the ontologists. It is just that while Canguilhem happily sided with epistemologists (he celebrated the indeterminacy of the world after ontology), the ontologists, as their name suggests, positioned themselves as critics of epistemology.

Take, for example, Annemarie Mol's The Body Multiple (2002), a study of how physicians with different clinical expertise (anatomy, internal medicine, radiology, etc.) in a Dutch hospital know and speak about arteriosclerosis.

The problem with "epistemology," Mol writes in the preface to her book, is that it "is concerned with reference: it asks whether representations of reality are accurate" (2002, vii). Epistemology, in other words, is implicitly suggesting a distinction between nature (composed of discrete, human independent objects or diseases, such as arteriosclerosis) and humans (who discover and know these objects/diseases). To Mol this distinction between nature and the human is an untenable reproduction of the great divide that is constitutive of modernity, a great divide that needs to be overcome and left behind.

What is Mol's alternative?

Her answer is: Practices. The background to this alternative is a discovery she made in the course of her fieldwork in a Dutch arteriosclerosis clinic. Following patients from one ward to another, Mol at one point noted that the ways in which different medical experts know and speak about arteriosclerosis not only differ wildly—but that they also don't add up to anything coherent. "A plaque cut out of an atherosclerosis artery is not the same entity as the problem a patient with atherosclerosis talks about in the consulting room, even though they are both called by the same name" (Mol 2002, vii).

Epistemologists, Mol concluded, are obviously misguided. They hold on, wrongly, to the idea that there is an objective reality out there.[46] What "is," one could summarize Mol, depends on the different practices in place to know. And as practices differ in various places (even in a single clinic), so does reality. Hence the title of her book, *The Body Multiple*.

"This is the plot of my philosophical tale," she summarizes her argument, "that ontology is not a given in the order of things, but that, instead, ontologies are brought into being, sustained, or allowed to wither away in common, day-to-day, practices" (6).

Ontology, then, is the study of the ontological productivity of practices.

The background to Mol's ontological critique of epistemology is a set of arguments first presented by Bruno Latour.[47] In his *Pandora's Hope* (1999), Latour had insisted that microbes didn't exist before Pasteur invented them.

"Did microbes exist before Pasteur? No, they did not exist before he came along" (145).

Latour's aim was provocation. He set out to mock all those naturalists who assumed that Pasteur had discovered a discrete natural entity that was sitting under his microscope, with a name tag around its neck that said "microbe," patiently waiting to be discovered.

As an alternative to such a neat nature/culture distinction—humans discovered the natural thing microbe—Latour invented a whole different way of thinking. What we have to learn, he explained to his readers, is that "the word 'substance' doesn't designate what 'remains beneath,' impervious to history" (1999, 151). Rather, the term "substance"—or being—refers to "what gathers together a multiplicity of agents into a stable and coherent whole" (151).

Latour's point is not that microbes are a human invention or a mere reflection of human practices. He doesn't say that Pasteur invented them from scratch. Rather, Latour suggests that what Pasteur refers to as microbes was impossible without a whole set of tools and actors on which they remain contingent: the microscope, Pasteur himself, the nascent public health movement, the Academy of Science, and many more.

Microbes, for Latour, are a node in an actor network on which they are contingent. They would not be without it—even if they are a constitutive part of it (this is a paradox that Latour has never sufficiently addressed: his alternative to epistemology remains as referential as epistemology). Or, in Latour's words, "Substance is a name that designates the stability of an assemblage" (1999, 151).[48]

Mol seems to have taken Latour's hilarious provocation literally—and thereby she deprived Latour of his ironic edge (to say that Latour's argument is ironic doesn't imply that he isn't serious). It is as if she humorlessly insists on an argument that Latour organized as a flirt—that microbes don't exist. Latour, grand maître of flirtation, was busy bringing about a situation in which one cannot decide whether or not he really means what he says. It is this openness on which the power of his argument depends. Mol, however, is decided: there is no such thing as microbes (or arteriosclerosis) independent of the practices in place to know microbes.

Ontology began as a dehumorization of Latour's work.[49]

What Eduardo Viveiros de Castro, Philippe Descola, and Eduardo Kohn share with Annemarie Mol is the reference to Latour's critique of epistemology, to his effort to radically abandon the nature/culture divide and think of the whole world in terms of actor networks and nature-culture hybrids.

The suggestion on behalf of the anthropologists here seems to be that Latour is right: that the split between humans (culture) and nature was a terrible mistake; that the societies anthropologists have studied have (always) known this (or, in any case, never have made the mistake); and that these societies—or at least their anthropologists (ethnographers)—can therefore teach us how to think of the world beyond the great divides that haunt the moderns.[50]

It is a bit as if Latour provided classical modern ethnography with a platform for presenting its own work as relevant to contemporary debates in STS and the human sciences more broadly.

What all the ontologists share, then—Latour, Mol, Viveiros de Castro, Descola, and Kohn—is a rejection of the joy of the irreducible openness (of the liberation) that is implicit in Canguilhem's celebration of epistemology. To various degrees, their project is to reestablish ontology over epistemology. And, thus, however implicitly, to reestablish the finiteness of the world (an ontology, even one that allows for difference/newness, can allow for difference/newness only insofar as it can be explained in terms of a general theory of being).

Call it a closure.

OBSERVATION 3

It seems to me as if one can distinguish three different lines of ontology. In my observation, neither one of these lines breaks with "the human."

First, there is the STS line, which emerged with Annemarie Mol and was later promoted by John Law; Bruno Latour has consistently flirted with this line (see, for example, Law and Lien 2013; for a critical review on ontology in STS, see Woolgar and Lezaun 2013; and Lynch 2013).

Is Mol's ontology after "the human"?

On the contrary. When what arteriosclerosis is—or whether it is at all—is completely contingent on how humans talk about it or enact it, then arteriosclerosis is, ultimately, a human invention. Mol's ontology thus amounts to a most radical anthropocentrism (what is more, it amounts to a dramatic overestimation of the significance of humans, an overestimation one could describe as key feature of modernity).[51]

Can as much be said of Latour's redefinition of "substance"?

I am inclined to think so. Of course, I am aware that there is no natural thing called a microbe, that microbe is a concept. Or, as Latour has brilliantly argued in *Science in Action* (1987), a list of propositions. However, there is a subtle but far-reaching difference between saying that microbes qua substance (however ill-defined) didn't exist before Pasteur—that they were *created* by him ex nihilo—and the suggestion that *for humans* microbes didn't exist, that what microbes are, for humans, depends on a complex set of experiments and tools and policies, that "microbe," of course, is a human word (and hence a mere contingency), and that given this dependency of human knowledge of microbes on tools and concepts microbes are inherently unstable entities (call it the distinction between creation and constitution).

The art of not being explicit doesn't solve the problem of reference: It therefore seems as if neither Latour nor Mol escapes the anthropocentrism that they problematize.[52]

The second line of ontological research emerges from the works of Eduardo Viveiros de Castro and Philippe Descola and could be called, in accordance with their self-descriptions, "comparative ontology."

Both Descola and Viveiros de Castro have repeatedly sought to define anthropology proper as the study of how societies (including Western society) construct the ontologies in which they are entangled. For example, Descola has consistently suggested "that conceptions of nature are socially constructed" and that anthropology should understand itself as the "comparative" study of these "socially constructed ontologies" (Descola 1996a, 82; 1996b; 2010a; 2010b; 2013; 2014). Similarly, Viveiros de Castro has argued that the task of anthropology is to compare the different ways in which societies "construct" the ontological worlds in which they are entangled, and to use these comparisons as a tool for translation, that is, to render different societies and their ontologies—to the degree that this is possible—comprehensible to one another (for example, see Viveiros de Castro 2004a, 2004b, 2014; see also Holbraad et al. 2014).

To both, the unit of analysis, in line with classical modern ethnography, are societies, understood as somewhat discrete, autonomous units (ethnoi).

At the center of the work of both Descola and Viveiros de Castro is a "discovery" that they have derived at, independently it seems, via their comparative ventures: while Western societies are human-exclusive—non–humans have no space—most (all?) non-Western societies have integrated nonhumans into their social world.[53]

It is on the basis of just this "discovery" that they have come to affirm Latour's critique of modernity: as the exclusion of nature from human sociality cannot be observed anywhere but in the modern West, it must be but one big mistake.

Conclusion: we have never been modern.

Arguably, this second line of ontological research is as little after "the human" as Mol's (or Latour's). Nor, for that matter, is it after ethnos. After all, it is humans that construct their worlds, whether they allow animals and plants to be part of them or not.

I reiterate that the concept of society is a distinctively modern one, invented to bring into view the uniqueness (in Diderot's sense) of the human. A yet to be written history of how society emerged as a quintessential—taken for granted—anthropological concept, would have to focus on at least three critical events.

First, in the decades leading up to the French Revolution, the ancient legal concept of societas was reconfigured by French authors as a revolutionary tool: the argument was that what is constitutive of a political unit is not the king and his court but rather society (which at that time simply meant the society of all those who held legal positions vis-à-vis the king). Second, after the French Revolution, humans were reconstituted as something they had never been before: social beings (note the difference between the aristocratic concept of sociality and the social). When, in the context of industrialization and the arrival of the first cholera epidemics from India, the French government charged statisticians to investigate patterns of poverty and disease, they discovered that where one was born, in which segment of society, determined one's life: what education one got, what job one was likely to have, how early one would marry (and whom), how many children one would have, what diseases one would suffer from, how long one would live. Third, based on social statistics, the idea emerged—the reference here is largely to Émile Durkheim—that societies really are organism like entities with a life of their own: individual human lives only seemed to be a matter of individual choice or free will.

In reality they were simply reflections of the structure and life stage of a given society. Durkheim's conclusion, famously, was that if one were to understand anything about the human, one would need a new kind of science, a social science, that would explore the social grounds constitutive of human exceptionalism.

Differently put, between the 1750s and the 1890s society and the social emerged as a radically new conceptual comprehension of the human—and of politics—one formerly unknown, one that marked (and still marks, despite its historical contingency) the condition of the possibility of the social sciences.

Of course, one could argue that the emergence of an anthropocentric, human-exclusive conception of society is simply a peculiarity of modern Western societies (whatever "West" might mean). But wouldn't such an argument silently reintroduce the concept of society as it has been constitutive of social anthropologies throughout the twentieth century, that is, as the invariable universal that allows a comparison of multiple ontologies? Indeed, wouldn't such an argument ultimately reintroduce the suggestion that humans—as members of society, as social beings—construct the (natural) worlds in which they live?

Instead of answering, I quote Descola (2013, xx):

> Anthropology is faced with a daunting challenge: either to disappear as an exhausted form of humanism or else to transform itself by rethinking its domain and its tools in such a way as to include in its object far more than the anthropos: that is to say, the entire collective of beings that is linked to him but is at present relegated to the position of a merely peripheral role; or, to put it in more conventional terms, the anthropology of culture must be accompanied by an anthropology of nature that is open to that part of themselves and the world that human beings actualize and by means of which they objectify themselves.

Humans actualize nature, use it to objectify themselves. How they do so differs from society to society.

Comparative ontology is hardly a move after "the human." On the contrary, it is (1) entirely contingent on / complicit with the modern plot, and (2) simply a continuation of the old social anthropology as it first emerged in the early twentieth century in France and the United Kingdom—with all of the distinctive features of "the human" as maker of the world. If what the world "is" is contingent on how human societies construct it, then what is this if not a reproduction of the anthropocentric epistemology that first emerged in the second half of the eighteenth century?[54]

The last line of ontology—the reference here is largely to Eduardo Kohn—is perhaps the most theoretically ambitious: Kohn's thought-provoking work revolves around the effort to articulate a theory of the ontological structure of the world as it exists as such.

Kohn's suggestion is that the natural world, the things of which it is composed of, have meaning as such, independent of the human. Indeed, he is adamant that plants and animals and clouds and the wind think, just like humans, and that each one of these natural instances is an active meaning producer, just like humans. In his work, which draws on his field-work in the Amazon, Kohn seeks to come up with a conceptual vocabu-lary that would allow modern humans to learn anew how to discover, to understand, and to live in this meaningful world that is, as Kohn puts it, beyond the human.

It seems to me as if this last line is not after "the human" either. On the surface of things, it may seem as if it goes further than the other two lines. For example, one could argue that Kohn, insofar as he brings the nonhu-man as such into view, as independent of humans, succeeds in decou-pling anthropological analysis from its focus on the human. However, the nonhuman actors about which Kohn writes seem all too human. Indeed, the vocabulary on which Kohn's universal ontology of the world beyond the human relies—its condition of possibility—is rather provincial: his ac-tors, humans and nonhumans alike, all come across as actors and mean-ing producers, and are all described in terms of the eighteenth-century vocabulary a rather small set of European authors invented to establish human exceptionalism.

Differently put, Kohn's project to make visible the ontological qual-ity of the nonhuman world as something in itself consists simply in the effort to expand the terms invented to set the human apart from the natural world to the natural world. The consequence could be described as a total "humanization" of the world (or as a radical universalization of "the human"); it leaves the eighteenth-century concept of "the human" unproblematized.[55]

Kohn's universalization of "the human," thus, is entirely contingent on (leaves in place) the anthropological discourse with which the anthropology "of" the human / after "the human" seeks to radically break.

His ontology is not after "the human." It is just beyond "the human."

(Occasionally it even seems as if Kohn's ontology privileges the human. For is it not humans who discover and articulate the ontological structure of the world?)

OBSERVATION 4

The perhaps most radical difference between an anthropology "of" the human / after "the human" and ontology is that the latter is, from the perspective of the former, a replacement approach. A central theme of the anthropology "of" the human is to break with "the human"—and to then maintain, to foster, the openness that emerges from this rupture and the indeterminacy—the many different, noncumulative, perhaps mutually exclusive indeterminacies—that emanates from it. A challenge that is built into this project is the courage to withstand situations of irreducible, nonteleological openness. To not close them: to enjoy them.

One could speak of a principle of radical disquiet, of ceaseless movement.

The aim of ontology is the inverse: the challenge it faces is to explain how the world "is." The challenge is—explicitly (Kohn, Latour) or implicitly (Descola, de Castro)—to advance a general ontological theory of how the world is built and to then think of the human as integrated into this world.

What is more, if ontologists critique the human—or nature/culture—then because it was "wrong," a mistake of an erroneous modern past, which needs to be corrected in the name of the truth (implying that they have broken through to the ontological structure of the world).

Latour is exemplary here. He effectively argues that the distinction between nature and culture has, insofar as it runs diagonal to how the world is, destroyed the world. Modernity, for Latour, amounts to a major mistake that urgently ought to be corrected. How? We all ought to learn to think in terms of Actor-Network Theory (ANT).

Ontology thus appears (or stylizes itself), however implicitly, as a breakthrough to the truth. As such it doesn't produce any openness at all—or only in an ontological sense, that is, by predefining what openness means in this world (even when it elaborates a concept of openness, it provides a definition of this openness and thereby—destroys it).

Let me add that occasionally, this new, better truth is morally charged: The suggestion is that "the human" has brought about the Anthropocene—and environmental pollution and mass species extinction—and that we humans now need to learn is to live beyond the human, to live in accordance with the natural world we are part of (see especially Descola 2013 and Kohn 2015, who both argue that in the age of climate change we moderns ought to learn how to live from societies who have not separated humans from the natural world).

This seems like a naïve return of eighteenth-century conceptions of the noble savage—a positive rearticulation of the classical theme of the philosophy of history: that the faraway, small-scale societies (from a European perspective) that anthropologists have traditionally studied are closer to nature than the modern European societies who have liberated themselves from the contingency of nature (see Lorraine Daston's brilliant 2004 critique of the moral authority of nature argument).

Along with this moral undertone often goes the celebration, on behalf of the ontologists, of some original (haptic) wisdom that the primitive has preserved and that the moderns (cool, rational, technicized, alienated from nature) have forgotten or lost (even though the haptic is arguably a modern concept).

It is occasionally difficult to avoid the impression that the ontological turn is a turn to (or return of) early twentieth-century primitivism: As a modernist celebration of the premodern, understood as the solution to the problems of modernity, ontology is a proper part of the epoch it so vehemently critiques.[56]

Let me add that multispecies anthropology often falls into a similar primitivist trap: just as classical modern ethnographers studied strange and exotic others—the "primitive," the "savage," with their seemingly inexplicable rituals—multispecies anthropologists study strange and exotic animals and their seemingly inexplicable (but endlessly curious) behavior.

And as the "primitive" was once invented—or instrumentalized—by ethnographers to put the taken-for-grantedness of our own, Western lifestyle in question, so today the animal is used to question our self-description as "human." What is more, just as every ethnographer once had her tribe, so each multispecies anthropologist has her animal or plant. There might be a focus on animals rather than on humans, but in a curious—problematic—turn, animals (or plants) often seem to assume the role formerly reserved to "the primitive": as a moralizer of the (Western, modern concept of the) human.[57]

OBSERVATION 5

Why ontology at all? Isn't the concern with "being" one of the Western obsessions par excellence?[58]

One could, for example, ask if there have been languages that don't have a word for being. Or forms of living in the world that escape the conception of being, which itself tends to inevitably introduce a form of universalism. Isn't being just another category that orders the world in a particular way?

If one wanted to address the question of radical alterity—my reference here is to Elizabeth Povinelli's work on the "otherwise" (2014, 2016) wouldn't one then need to venture "after" ontology? Rather than articulate an (however alternative) ontology? The challenge would be to build "derangements" without referring to "the plane of existence" (Povinelli 2014).

I think, for example, of Emmanuel Levinas's vehement critique of ontology as violence in *Otherwise than Being, or Beyond Essence* (1981). Or of Gilles Deleuze's radical departure from *all* ontologies.

"Philosophy," Deleuze suggested in a conversation with Claire Parnet (1977, 56), "is encumbered with the problem of being." Everything, he laments, revolves around "the verb *to be*." His alternative was to instead focus on relations. The goal, he told Parnet (ed.), is to show that "relations are an autonomous sphere, distinct from . . . existence." What is more, we have to learn to see that "relations are external to their terms! . . . We have to make the encounter with relations penetrate and corrupt everything, undermine being, topple it over. Substitute the AND for IS. A and B. The

AND is not even a specific relation or conjunction, it is that which subtends all relations, the path of all relations, which make relations shoot outside their terms and outside the set of their terms, and outside everything which could be determined as Being, One, or Whole. The AND as extra-being."[59] Deleuze insists that it is naïve to assume that a multiplicity—a thing—"is defined by its elements. What defines it [instead]," he insists, "is the AND, as something which has its place between the elements or between the sets. AND, AND, AND. . . . Things do not begin to live except in the middle."

I wish to state clearly that I have no interest in deriving a program from Deleuze, let alone in ontologizing his philosophy of the AND.

If I quote Deleuze's reflection, it is solely because the French philosopher problematizes the focus on "being"—and, hence, the obsession with ontology—to such a degree that the focus on being loses its self-evidence, with the consequence that it becomes possible to wonder out loud if there are actually escapes from being: escapes to be found through the surprise-producing practice called fieldwork/research.

Could anthropologies after ethnos free the human—the world—from the grip of the verb "to be"? Could anthropologists learn to think in terms of the middle? Without making the mistake of ontologizing relations?[60]

What is at stake in asking these questions is *not* the call for a new general theory of relations (or, even worse, an ontology of relations). What is at stake, rather, is to expose and question the verb "to be" and to thereby open up possibilities for inquiries that are not focused on being (not even in terms of becoming or in terms of a historical ontology); inquiries that are not conducted to authorize truth claims in terms of being/becoming; inquiries that are sensitive to what one could, perhaps, call the always singular, always irreducible difference between "things" and "being."[61]

It might be that every AND is different—so that any ontology of the AND would fail. Always. So that the task would be to expose oneself and to explore the precise forms of these failures. Endlessly.

It matters to me to cut loose—to differentiate and to liberate—the study of the nonhuman, natural world from the hegemony of ontology. Why? Because I wish to maintain the incredibly dynamic openness that the expansion of anthropological inquiry into the natural world is capable of provoking.

3

on fieldwork

(itself)

ONE

Most anthropologists take it for granted—and it indeed sounds obvious—that fieldwork and ethnography are really synonyms: to be an anthropologist is to conduct fieldwork, and to conduct fieldwork is to conduct ethnography.

I am interested in the historicity of this taken-for-grantedness.

When did it become obvious that doing fieldwork meant to do ethnography? And why? What event—or what series of events—led to the self-evident equation of fieldwork with ethnography? Can one write the history of this self-evidence?

If I raise the question concerning the relation between fieldwork and ethnography, it is not least because I am curious about what one could call the possibility of "fieldwork after ethnos" (and after "the human"). I wonder what happens to fieldwork when anthropologists no longer study ethnos or conduct ethnographies? What is the role of fieldwork—if any—when cut loose (liberated) from the study or society and/or culture?[1]

Differently put, I am interested in the fragility of the equation of fieldwork with ethnography. And my aim is to exploit this fragility.

TWO

Let's begin with conceptual history. Where do the terms "ethnography" and "fieldwork" come from? When do they first appear? Who used them? To what ends?

The term "ethnography" appeared in the late eighteenth century to introduce a new subclass of geographical research. Probably the first to use the term was Gerhard Philipp Heinrich Normann (1753–1837), a German *Staatswissenschaftler* and statistician. Normann suggested that geography came in one of three forms: mathematical geography, physical geography, or political geography. Ethnography he defined as a subclass of political geography.[2]

I thus note that the term "ethnography" was originally introduced to refer to a practice—a curiosity—that belongs to the broad field of natural history.

The term "fieldwork" is of much more recent datum. With respect to anthropology it was first used (in a systematic sense at least) in the early twentieth century, in the writings of British social anthropologists—I notably found the term in the writings of Bronisław Malinowski (1884–1942) and his students—who sought to methodologically ground ethnography.

"Fieldwork" emerged as a qualifier of "ethnography."

What event, though, or what trajectory of events, led Malinowski and his students to argue, with vehemence, that the only proper form of ethnography was fieldwork? And what did they mean by "ethnography," what by "fieldwork"?

My research led me to think that the condition of the possibility for the encounter between ethnography and fieldwork was prepared gradually, in complicated, haphazard, and unintentional ways, in the period between the late 1890s and the early 1920s.

There was nothing straightforwardly obvious about this encounter. The concept of fieldwork-based ethnography wasn't a future anticipated in the past—a vanishing point that teleologically organized the history of anthropological research and that eventually resulted in a breakthrough to the truth. On the contrary, it was an unanticipated—a sweeping—event, one for which many contemporaries were unprepared, one that radically reconfigured what anthropology in theory and practice was about.

Up until the late nineteenth century, anthropological research came in roughly one of two forms—expeditions to (from a European perspective) faraway lands or the largely home-based reconstruction of various features of the early history of what was then called "mankind."[3]

Expeditions. In its modern sense as "journey undertaken by a group of people with a scientific or explorative purpose," the term "expedition" emerged only at the turn from the sixteenth to the seventeenth century.[4] Initially, it referred to voyages undertaken with an interest in discovering unknown lands for economic purposes (think, for example, of the travels that led to the British East India Company).[5] Beginning in the middle of the eighteenth century, the term was increasingly used for scientific explorations, specifically for the cartographical mapping of coastlines and geographical surveys of the flora and fauna of unknown regions of the earth. The exemplary reference here is to Captain Cook's voyages in the Pacific Ocean (1768–71, 1772–75, and 1776–79).[6] At the turn from the eighteenth to the nineteenth century, European expeditions then shifted focus and targeted primarily South America (think Alexander von Humboldt) and inner Africa (think David Livingston). And in the late nineteenth century, finally, the North and South Pole were explored (recall that Franz Boas, in 1883, went to Baffin Island as a geographer).[7]

What form did anthropological knowledge production take during these expeditions?

Usually the expeditions included young scholars and artists trained as botanists or physicians—figures such as Johann Foster (1729–1798) and Georg Forster (1754–1794), members of Captain Cook's second voyage, and heroes of von Humboldt and Boas—who became curious about the "savages" and began documenting aspects of their lifestyle. The form this documentation took was the one they, as zoologists and botanists, had available: they sketched (and occasionally also measured) the physiognomies of the people they visited, just as they sketched the plants and birds they encountered; they draw up maps of the architecture and of the villages; they collected, mostly in an unsystematic, random fashion, material goods and myths and songs; and, occasionally, they also captured people and sent them home for further examination and exhibition.[8]

Reconstruction. Next to the expeditions, there were the armchair reconstructions of the early history of mankind. It is interesting to compare the authors of these reconstructions—for example, Robert Latham (1812–1888), John McLennan (1827–1881), Johann Jakob Bachofen (1815–1887), Friedrich Müller (1834–1898), and Henry Maine (1822–1888)—with the collectors who joined expeditions.

If the latter were overwhelmingly naturalists, trained in botany or zoology (or science more generally), then the former were overwhelmingly philologists, experts in the interpretation of ancient texts and artifacts (or philologically inclined jurists, who studied antiquity to understand the early legal organization of society).

It is not that the philologists didn't travel. However, their professional travels did not lead them to small islands in the Pacific Ocean. As experts on antiquity—in the nineteenth century almost synonymous with "expert on the early history of mankind"—they voyaged to Greece or Rome or Egypt or Persia. And in their efforts to reconstruct various features of the ancient world, from myths to marriage rules (from property rights to political systems), they got interested in the savages as a group of people that would allow them to understand the prehistory that led from a somewhat animal-like existence to antiquity—and thus began to turn to the collections of texts and artifacts provided by the naturalist travelers. Several among the philologists also developed an elaborate correspondence with missionaries and salesmen spread out across the British Empire (one could easily write a media-history of early British anthropology: showing how anthropology was contingent on a tightly knit network of correspondence that unfolded alongside the extraordinary infrastructural expansion of British Royal Mail over the course of the eighteenth and nineteenth century).

Although brief, my sketch of the emergence and development of forms of anthropological knowledge productions allows me to draw two conclusions.

First, beginning in the late eighteenth century, with the success of Captain Cook's voyages, one can see the gradual emergence and consolidation of what was an anthropological curiosity in its own right (as the emergence and quick spread of the term "ethnography" shows).

Second, even though anthropology emerged as a curiosity in its own right, at the end of the nineteenth century, it had still not emerged as an autonomous, distinctive genre of knowledge production; it had not yet differentiated itself, either methodologically or conceptually, from natural history on the one hand (zoology, botany, geography), and universal history on the other.

Thus the form anthropology took by the 1890s was ethnography. And the term "ethnography" referred to either the collection of artifacts in the tradition of naturalism or the interpretation of artifacts in the tradition of philology. While the philologists partly drew on the work of the naturalists, the two forms of expertise were largely set apart from one another.

The event that would prepare the possibility for this nineteenth-century conception of anthropology—of ethnography—to break open was yet another expedition: the 1898–99 Cambridge expedition to the Torres Strait.[9]

FOUR

The Cambridge Anthropological Expedition to the Torres Strait was designed and directed by Alfred C. Haddon (1855–1940), a zoologist who specialized in marine life forms. In the late 1880s, Haddon, at that time professor of zoology in Dublin, had joined an expedition that aimed to explore the flora and fauna of the area between New Guinea and Australia referred to as the Torres Strait. His specific task was the study of life around coastal coral reefs. It was while standing knee-deep in the ocean collecting algae that Haddon became curious about anthropology (Haddon et al. 1935, xi):

> I was in close contact with the islanders, especially when dredging and collecting algae. Naturally, when opportunity offered, I spoke with them about their past and soon found that the young men knew extremely little about it and always referred me to the old men. I had previously found that none of the Europeans in the island knew or cared anything about the customs of the natives. . . . I therefore considered it my duty to collect as much as was possible . . . , so I induced the old men to come in the evenings and talk about old times and tell me their folk-tales.

After his return to the United Kingdom, Haddon began writing anthropology papers—and sought to convince colleagues of the necessity of a carefully planned scientific expedition that would systematically study the life and customs of the islanders of the Torres Strait. Haddon was plagued by a sense of urgency: he had no doubt that civilization would destroy the ancient societies forever, and his plan was to collect their folk tales, take pictures of their rituals, record their songs, film their ceremonies, and systematically collect material artifacts.[10]

In 1898, Haddon finally found a donor, and the expedition took off. Aside from Haddon, the crew was composed of Sydney H. Ray (1858–1939, a philologist) and Charles Seligman (1873–1940, a physician who studied native medicine), as well as William Halse Rivers Rivers (1864–1922), William McDougall (1871–1938), and Charles S. Meyers (1873–1946) (three physicians and psychologists who were charged to study "the mental characteristics of primitive people"; Meyers also documented native instruments and music), and Anthony Wilkin (1871–1901, an archeologist).

On the one hand, the voyage to the Torres Strait was little more than yet another nineteenth-century expedition. Haddon had designed the journey as if it were a botanical or zoological trip: the aim was to survey and to collect—to collect specimens that one could arrange and rearrange back home, thereby carefully reconstructing the early evolution of mankind.

On the other hand, the expedition was a most powerful departure from its predecessors: while almost every other scientific expedition of the nineteenth century was focused on a broad set of naturalistic curiosities, from cartography to astronomy, from botany to ethnography, Haddon had organized his voyage exclusively around anthropological questions: the salvaging of the disappearing culture of the primitives. A hardly ever noticed but retrospectively far-reaching consequence of this exclusive focus was the transfer of a vocabulary initially developed for studies in natural history to anthropology. Indeed, it was only with the Cambridge Anthropological Expedition to the Torres Strait that, however implicitly, the assumption emerged that anthropology was a "field science"—a field science in its own right, independent from natural history.[11]

FIVE

Among the younger members of Haddon's team, the experience of "the field," coupled with the exclusive focus on anthropological questions, led to an awareness of how far off were the speculations of the philologists (and jurists) about primitives. Charles Seligman and Rivers in particular stressed upon their return to England that any future anthropology had to be understood as a field science, that is, it had to be grounded in firsthand empirical research experience.

Differently put, they sought to ground the reconstructive efforts of the philologists and lawyers in the expedition-based knowledge of the field.

As if to prove their point, both Seligman and Rivers, independently from one another, undertook a whole series of further anthropological researches.

ON FIELDWORK 75

Seligman first worked in New Guinea, as member of the Daniel Ethnographical Expedition (which resulted in his *Melanesians of British New Guinea*, 1910), and then, together with his wife, Brenda Seligman, undertook government-sponsored survey studies of Ceylon (*The Veddas*, 1911) and the Sudan (*The Pagan Tribes of the Nilotic Sudan*, 1932).[12]

While Seligman's work remained much indebted to nineteenth-century conceptions of ethnography—he may have stressed "the field," but the field mattered only insofar as it allowed for the empirically saturated classification of "races" and the comparison of customs—Rivers's continued anthropological research led him to articulate a whole new set of questions.

During the Torres Strait expedition, one of Rivers's tasks had been to study the prevalence of color blindness among the islanders. Curious about hereditary patterns, he asked his interlocutors about their genealogical relations and thus discovered, more by chance than by design, the extraordinary richness of the islanders' kinship vocabulary.[13] Confronted with the suggestion that people had several fathers and mothers, he worked out for himself a genealogical method that allowed him to reconstruct "blood ties" versus "affiliation" and "adoption" (his terms).[14] When in 1901 and 1902 he worked among the Todas (living in the Nilgiri Mountains of Southern India), Rivers, sensitized to and curious about the rich relational vocabulary of non-Western people, recognized the significance of kinship ties for understanding what he called "the system of relations" that seemed to silently organize who was responsible for the different elements of a given ceremony (*The Todas*, 1906).[15]

Could he draw up this system? And thereby explain the structure of the life of the Todas?

Perhaps one has to pause for a moment to appreciate how form-giving Rivers's "discovery" has been: his recognition of the organization of the whole of social life in terms of kinship in 1901–2 is one of the key moments in the history that would eventually lead to the emergence of classical modern ethnography, understood as the fieldwork-based study of a single society (ethnos) and its internal social structure.[16] As long as customs were specimens to be collected and shipped home, an island-hopping expedition was an adequate form of anthropological research. However, once customs were windows onto the lived enactment of the structure that silently organized the living together of individuals, a new, and in the early twentieth century yet undefined and unknown, form of research was needed.

Rivers was acutely aware of the need for methodological innovation. He knew that merely stressing the importance of "the field" was not enough.

What was needed, in addition, was a new definition of what anthropology was about.

Rivers's most explicit effort to provide such a definition was his contribution to the edition of the *Notes and Queries* issued by the Royal Anthropological Institute in 1912. There he first affirmed that the goal of anthropology is, ultimately, to collect data that would eventually allow one to understand the early history of mankind (Rivers would always hold on to this nineteenth-century conception of anthropology).[17] But he then went ahead and wondered out loud if this overall goal wouldn't require carefully studying single societies and the system of relations that organize them, so that one could then later conduct a comparative study of their structure of organization. Indeed, Rivers not only recommended to future anthropologists that they study one society at a time but also encouraged them to study how the natives who belong to these societies actually see the world.

In a passage that (still) reads like an avant-garde program of experimental research, he wrote (I quote at length),

> Above all, never neglect a statement volunteered by a witness independently. . . . Leave the main path of the inquiry and follow this side track. If the volunteered statement is obscure or even quite unintelligible, so much the better; it may and probably does mean that you have been put on a track which will lead to something absolutely new and unsuspected, while your main path was probably leading to some goal already more or less understood and foreseen. . . . To many it will be repugnant; the person with an "orderly mind" who believes in probing one subject to the bottom before turning elsewhere and cannot suffer interruption in his train of thought, will miss much. He will probably complain bitterly of the difficulty of keeping the people to the point, not recognizing that the native also has a point, probably of far more interest than his own. Further, such information is of very great value as evidence, for it is certain to follow the native categories of thought.[18]

In the early 1920s, two young anthropologists who had worked with Seligman and with Rivers in particular presented the first empirical studies of a single society.

Alfred Reginald Radcliffe-Brown's (1881–1955) *The Andaman Islanders* (1922) was thoroughly indebted to Rivers's systems approach. Radcliffe-Brown presented his study—which was grounded in repeated, expedition-like trips to "the field"—as an almost mathematical inquiry into social organization typical of a group at the very beginning of the history of mankind, at a time when neither government nor property were yet known.[19]

Bronisław Malinowski, though much influenced by both Seligman and Rivers, radically broke with the vision of anthropology upheld by his teachers.[20] He presented his *Argonauts of the Western Pacific* (1922) as the beginning of an altogether new kind of anthropology, one that was grounded in what he called "fieldwork" and that aimed to provide a description of the "inner life of a society."[21]

Malinowski styled his work as a sweeping departure from the nineteenth century. He ridiculed the island-hopping of the naturalists and in particular the armchair speculations of the philologists (and lawyers). Their speculations on this myth or that ritual, he explained to his perplexed readers, tell us more about the authors who offer them than about the actual life of the primitives.[22] Instead of speculating, the task of the "ethnographer" was to carefully study the role that a given custom or myth or material artifact played "inside" of a given society. Everything the natives did, Malinowski insisted, had its "function" or "meaning." And the only way to understand this meaning (function) was to conduct "fieldwork," that is, to learn the language, to take part in the everyday life of the natives, living among them, in their midst, "without other white men." The challenge was to immerse oneself in "the imponderabilia of everyday life" and to abstract from them the "underlying ideas" that organize the actions of the primitives.[23]

The significance of Malinowski for the history I try to write is that he— and with him his many students who conducted "fieldwork-based ethnography"—succeeded in decoupling "ethnography" from both evolutionary speculations and speculative reconstructions of the early history of mankind. His alternative was the inseparable correlation of ethnography—defined and practiced by him as the description of the inner life and organization of a society— and fieldwork.

Differently put, Malinowski invented—in a sweeping coup—what became self-evident in the course of the twentieth century: that anthropology is fieldwork is ethnography.[24] Most critical for this becoming self-evident was the first cohort of Malinowski's students, who made ethnography—fieldwork— the state-of-the-art method of anthropology. The reference is to Raymond Firth (1901–2002), Audrey Richard (1899–1984), Hortense Powdermaker (1896–1970), Isaac Schapera (1905–2003), Edward E. Evans-Pritchard (1902–1973), and Meyer Fortes (1906–1983), among others.[25]

And Radcliffe-Brown?

If Radcliffe-Brown likened anthropology to a natural science busy describing social structures in the abstract, Malinowski likened anthropology to the arts—the challenge was to immerse oneself in the everyday life of a particular group; to discover, by way of attending to their conversations and habits, the "underlying ideas" that structure the natives' lives; and to then learn how to vividly describe, as a novelist describes (as a painter paints) the life of the primitive in such a way that the underlying ideas are rendered visible in the concrete—without rescue into the abstraction.[26]

If Radcliffe-Brown had taken from Rivers the interest in social evolution and systems of relations, then Malinowski took from Rivers the suggestion that "the native also has a point"—and that this point was implicit in his actions. For Malinowski, "the final goal, of which an ethnographer never should lose sight," was "to grasp the native point of view, his relation to life, to realize his vision of his world. We have to study man, and we have to study what concerns him most intimately, that is, the hold which life has on him."[27]

———

Do I really mean to suggest that anthropologists did not conduct fieldwork prior to the 1920s? No, if by "fieldwork" one merely means that someone has lived for a limited amount of time elsewhere and has written about her observations. Yes, if by "fieldwork" one means the disruptive methodological conception of research that emerged over the first two decades of the twentieth century and that forever changed what anthropology is about.[28]

SIX

What has been the effect of the emergence, since the late 1990s, of anthropologies after ethnos on the conception of "fieldwork as ethnography" as it was first articulated in the 1920s?

Differently put, what new, what other concepts of fieldwork have emerged from, say, studies of immunosuppressants (Lawrence Cohen 2001), Anonymous (Gabriella Coleman 2013), neoliberal city planning (Stephen Collier 2011), marine microbes (Stefan Helmreich 2009), influenza (Celia Lowe 2010; Carlo Caduff 2010, 2015), Chernobyl (Adriana Petryna 2002), open-source code (Christopher Kelty 2009), Matsutake (Anna Tsing 2015), life in vitro (Hannah Landecker 2000, 2002), bioprospecting (Cori Hayden 2003), AIDS (João Biehl 2007), cheese making (Heather Paxson 2012), monkeys (Nicolas Langlitz n.d.), curation (Tarek Elhaik 2016), basic income grants (James Ferguson 2015), cinema (Anand Pandian 2015), and censorship (William Maz-zarella 2013)?[29]

While it is difficult, and also unwarranted, to provide a single answer to the question of what fieldwork after ethnos is about—too wild, too untamed, are the still nascent fields of the anthropology after ethnos—it seems that one aspect many of the above-cited studies are concerned with is "difference in time."

In my schematic rendering, if anthropology in its form of classical modern ethnography was interested in difference in space—in distant others, their al-ternative social structure and cultural logic—then many of the anthropologies after ethnos seem to have replaced this classical interest in spatial difference with an intense curiosity about difference in time.

No longer does the anthropologist after ethnos ask "How is it elsewhere?" Instead she wonders out loud if something new/different has occurred—an event that set in motion a given domain of the real, that changed it, mutated it beyond recognition, an event that challenges the constitution of the real as we know it as well as the conceptions of the human that lay dormant therein.[30]

What is the effect of this interest in "difference in time" on the spatial category of the field? Why and to what ends does one conduct fieldwork when one is no longer conducting ethnography? What notion of the field, what concept of anthropology as a field science—if any—has emerged from the multitudinous, fieldwork-based studies of difference in time?[31]

SEVEN

In my observation, the anthropology interested in difference in time—in "events" and "the emergent"—is as radically a field science as has been the anthropology interested in difference in space. It upholds, like its more clas-sical sister variant, the primacy of the field, the field's particular potential to lead astray, to profoundly derail the research questions one has laid out before one entered the field—and to thereby produce surprise.[32]

Fieldwork, for both classical modern ethnography and the anthropology after ethnos, is a powerful derailment machine, an opportunity to use the ac-cidental as a tool for unanticipated discoveries.

However, where research into that which is only emerging differs from fieldwork as we know it—where it has provoked a powerful mutation of the idea of a field science, of what it is and what it is after—is that derailment is set to radically different use.

For the more classically oriented anthropologists, that is, for those primarily interested in spatial difference (how people live elsewhere), the concept of derailment (most often) refers to the accumulative experience that one's own presuppositions—including those one did not even know about—are different from those made by the group of people one studies. The methodological significance of this experience is its enabling character—it enables the anthropologist to become (often through serendipitous accidents) aware of the presuppositions others make.

It follows that anthropologists usually assume, first, that a different set of underlying ideas organizes the lives of others (which implies that these "other ideas"—even if they are nowhere explicitly articulated—objectively exist out there, almost in the form of discrete entities to be discovered), and second, that derailment amounts to a kind of rerailment, a being rerailed to precisely those ideas that organize the culture or society (or the social or cultural phenomenon) one studies.

Rivers's above-quoted suggestion to follow "volunteered statements," even if they "lead astray," is a case in point: according to Rivers, this being led "astray" is a sure path to the discovery of "the native's categories of thought" (one could also mention here Malinowski's [1922] talk about "underlying ideas" or Geertz's [1973] suggestion that unarticulated "scripts" organize the native's life).

The significance of an anthropology interested in difference in time—in the conceptual turbulences provoked by the new/different—is that it has radically broken with both these assumptions. To be more precise, it has decoupled derailment—the loss of orientation that results from the recognition that one's presuppositions don't work—from the idea of a rerailment. For where one inquires into that which is only emerging (or not even that yet), into that which comes into existence only at the moment of fieldwork, into that which is such that it escapes the already thought and known, there can be, strictly speaking, nothing one could be rerailed to. Research into the emergent is, quite literally, research into the open (even if the open occurs in very concrete fields and forms).

Like a well, the new/different springs forth, bifurcates in all directions, is explorative, perhaps wild, almost certainly chaotic and incoherent; it likely has not yet given rise to a broad stream in a stable riverbed—and maybe it never will, for it may just as well ooze out and disappear.

The very aim of studying events that open up a difference in time is quite literally to capture the openings, the bifurcations, the troubles, the jumping forth, the new causes. At stake is to capture "instances of escape," that is, situations in which the established breaks open. At stake as well is a continuous derailment by the unexpected ways and forms the new takes. Consequently, fieldworkers interested in the emergent are unlikely to be rerailed—for their goal is to be gripped by instances of derailment.[33]

Would it be a gross exaggeration, then, to suggest that the focus on "difference in time" has cut fieldwork loose from ethnography? And that the unanticipated consequence of this liberation has been that fieldwork has emerged as something in itself?

Today, fieldwork is no longer just a means to get at something that is more or less independent of it—the "underlying ideas" that supposedly structure the native's life. Instead it is an artful—experimental—technique at the core of which are accidents that have the power to disrupt the taken for granted. To be more precise, that have the power to open up unanticipated, still emergent spaces of marvel and surprise for which no one has words or concepts yet.

———

In chapter 1, I used the term "philosophical"—or "philosophically inclined"—anthropology. As I see it, the cutting loose of "fieldwork" from "ethnography" opens up a whole new set of possibilities for encounters between anthropology and art: Would it be saying too much to suggest that the possibilities of an empirically grounded, fieldwork-based philosophy I try to bring into view with this book—its focus on the accidental, its ventures into the irreducibly open, its curiosity about emergent forms, its celebration of movement / in terms of movement, its interest in escapes—offers a multitude of unanticipated interfaces between art and anthropology (between [some] artists and [some] philosophically inclined anthropologists)? Or that, on the level of technologies, vast, yet-to-be-explored venues for conversations and collaborations open up?[34]

EIGHT

There has been the occasional critique that when anthropologists entered labs, clinics, urban planning offices, and advertisement companies, and thus moved closer to cultural studies, science and technology studies, feminism, and theory- and history-inspired modes of inquiry, the power of the field got abandoned and eventually dried up.

I find such an argument utterly misleading. One may certainly argue that the rise to dominance of an anthropology of things modern has outgrown classical conceptions of the field. Who would doubt that? But it would be spectacularly wrong to assume that the process of outgrowing traditional conceptions of fieldwork as ethnography has implied the end of fieldwork.[35] In fact, I would argue that the exact opposite has been the case: since the 1990s the practice of fieldwork has proliferated in hitherto unknown ways. Anthropologists have transformed countless sites into fields that were once thought to be far beyond the scope of the discipline.

In short, over the last twenty years or so fieldwork has not disappeared—instead anthropologists have spectacularly expanded the possibility of conducting fieldwork. Indeed, in many ways, fieldwork—fieldwork itself—is more alive and well today than ever before.

Perhaps it has never been so exciting and extraordinary, never been so curious and creatively challenging to practice a field science as it is today.

———

Do I seriously mean to suggest that when one studies rituals in India, one studies space, but if one studies science in Monterey, one studies time? Am I not, thereby, however implicitly, reintroducing the old nineteenth-century European equations of spatial with temporal difference? Worse, am I not suggesting that those "still" living in or bound by "space" have not yet entered "history," that is, "time?"

I don't think so. The point I seek to make is that many of the anthropological studies that have been published since the early 2000s—whether focused on rituals in India or science in Monterey—did not so much ground in a spatial curiosity (How is it in India? How in California?) as in a temporal curiosity: what kinds of rituals has the Partition introduced to India? What new conceptions of evolution has the microbiology conducted in Monterey opened up?

What defines the focus of the study is less (not primarily) place than—a difference in time.

assemblages (or how to study difference in time?)

If the analytical vocabulary anthropology provided traditionally to its practitioners was designed to bring into view spatial differences, and if at least some anthropologists have broken with this focus on difference in space and replaced it with an interest in difference in time—then what new kind of analytical tools and concepts have these anthropologists of temporal difference come up with?

How can one bring into view—how can one analytically, through fieldwork, get a hold of—difference in time?

There are obvious candidates for answering this question. For example, over the last two decades anthropologists have in particular used the concept of the "event" and "the emergent" to capture temporal differences.[36] Equally prominent have been the concept of the "contemporary" or of "the recent past and the near future."[37] Here, however, I want to focus on an altogether different concept, "assemblages."[38]

My reference is less to the work of Gilles Deleuze and Félix Guattari (whose use of the term *agencement* in *Mille plateaux* Brian Massumi once translated as "assemblage") than to a fragment from a conversation between Bruno Latour and Michel Serres.[39]

How come, Latour wants to know from Serres, you treat long-dead authors as contemporaries?

"In order to say contemporary," Serres replies, "one must already be thinking of a certain time and thinking of it in a certain way.... So, let's put the question differently: What things are contemporary? Consider a late model car. It is a disparate aggregate of scientific and technical solutions dating from different periods. One can date it component by component: this part was invented at the turn of the century, another ten years ago, and Carnot's cycle is almost two hundred years old.... The ensemble is only contemporary by assemblage, by its design, its finish."[40]

The ensemble is contemporary only by *assemblage*.

Implicit in this formulation is an entire heuristic vocabulary for thinking about time in general and about difference in time in particular. Serres, however indirectly, suggests that any one moment in time, every instance of a here and now, ought be thought of as a temporal composite—as a *form* composed of different (disparate) elements moving in time. Almost as if he were saying, "Imagine the present as a *punctum*, a snapshot of the configuration between independent, freely moving elements at a given moment. Imagine further that each one of these elements has its own history, its own line of flight, its own speed, and that the connections between different elements, in itself perhaps a chance event, structures what is possible to think and say."

To speak of an assemblage, one thus could say, is to relate to the present—or some tiny part of it—as if it were a form-in-motion composed of a set of different elements (these can be concepts, practices, institutions, machines, technologies or people and other things). One could analyze each element of this form-in-motion separately (where it came from, how it developed). One could trace their individual histories, the speed with which they traveled (some are presumably faster, others slower), the assemblages they were part of in the past (and maybe still are), and the relations they formed. Or one could analyze the history of the relations between elements, that is, how they built up over time, how they changed, how they became denser or looser, or how the arrival of a new element reconfigured all relations and thereby gave the assemblage a new, unanticipated dynamic. One could also analyze the rate(s) at which individual elements—or the entire assemblage—mutate.

Take, for example, avian flu.

What a curious—and deadly—assemblage, composed of a long list of heterogeneous elements: viruses (as such), poultry farms, the history of domestication, biology, birds, migration routes, nesting grounds, rivers and lakes, humans, veterinarians, public health, drug companies, and so on.[41]

Arguably, the migration routes of birds and drug companies have hardly ever been thought of as related, nor have the straightening and regulation of rivers and poultry farms. And yet, the hopping of a virus between different species connected these—and many more elements than I list here—into a closely knit and intricately entangled assemblage that is constitutive of avian flu.

In the case of avian flu, thus, the emergence of an assemblage where before all there was were loosely (if at all) related lines of flight amounts to a massive event.

Disclaimer.

If I ponder Serres's reflections here, it is not because I think "Michel Serres got it right." Frankly, I don't know—and also don't care—if Serres got it right. What interests me here is not truth but rather possibility: the possibility of abstracting from a chance formulation—the ensemble is only contemporary by assemblage—a heuristically useful analytical vocabulary for an anthropological study of temporal difference.[42]

What follows are three brief (and tentative) entries that elaborate on what I mean by "heuristically useful."

First, the heuristic value of the concept of an assemblage is that it brings the present—understood as a moment in time—into view as composed of con-temporary elements (an assemblage), each with its distinctive moment of origin (some older, some more recent), each moving at a different speed—with different kinds of velocity—in different directions (and each element could be decomposed itself into an assemblage of sorts, made up of different kinds of elements, with different origins, and so on).

One primary effect of this rendering of a given moment in time (the here and now) as composed of moving elements is that it makes available to anthropologists an exuberantly rich vocabulary that is usually associated with the field of art, from music to painting to photography: composition, pace, movement, configuration, line of flight, directionality, dynamics, mutation, and speed.

One can now, for example, listen to Bach's *Art of Fugue* and begin to wonder—qua anthropologist of the here and now, qua de- and re-composer of the movements that make up the present—how one could single out among the many elements (each an instance of movement) one has listed in one's notebook just two in order to show how they ceaselessly circle one another, thereby producing the distinctive rhythm of (one segment of) life today.

Or one can look at the photography Étienne-Jules Marey—each a snapshot of movement, of the unfolding of time captured as motion— and wonder what one can learn, for example, from his rendering of the flight of a seagull for the analysis of different time lines of the elements of an assemblage.

FIG. 3.1 Johann Sebastian Bach, *Art of Fugue*, 1751. What can one learn, as field-working anthropologist concerned with instances of time composed of lines of flight, from Bach about analyzing assemblages? Could one translate the velocity of the different kinds of elements of an assemblage into a melody? H. and Fr. Rungs Music Archive, Royal Danish Library, Copenhagen.

Or one can look at the paintings of Paul Klee, who continuously described his art as an analysis of the ceaseless, inexhaustible movement and becoming implicit in plants and animals, in humans and things—as the practice of isolating the elements of this movement/becoming and of recomposing them into possible and yet unknown figures, figures that no one had ever seen.

Once one operates, on a heuristic level, with the term assemblage a whole new (and largely unanticipated) set of analytical vocabularies for an analysis of movement/in terms of movement becomes available.

What would it take to come up with a compositional analysis of the present? With a decoding of lines of flight in a tonal analysis? With a typography of possible kinds of movement? With an art history of the forms relations can take?[43]

Second, the concept of assemblage leaves behind the figure of "the human" and along with it what I have called (chapter 2) the "anthropocentric epistemology" on which anthropology had been built.

FIG. 3.2 Étienne-Jules Marey, *Analysis of the Flight of a Seagull*, 1887. Could one equally transform the line of flight—the time line—of an element of an assemblage into a linear series of photos—or of letters, words, sentences, paragraphs, texts? Etienne-Jules Marey/Dépot du Collège de France, Musée Marey, Beaune, France.

Take avian flu again: humans, birds, nesting grounds, laboratories, governments, migration routes, rivers, livestock, viruses, culling machines— are these vertical slices of the real, to borrow a phrase from Sandra Hyde (2007), human or nonhuman? Are they natural or cultural?[44]

Or take swine flu (substitute birds with pigs); or MERS (camels); Ebola (bats); or SARS (palm civets and/or raccoon dogs).[45]

Who is the author of these configurations?

Anna Tsing's suggestive answer to this question is that assemblages are by and large chance assemblies that exceed any form of human intentionality. Assemblages, consequently, are marked by "patterns of unintentional coordination." They are "open-ended gatherings" which potentially become "happenings" (as when, for example, a virus hops from birds—or pigs, camels, bats, palm civets—to humans).[46]

The assemblage concept—a bit like Althusser's reinterpretation of historical materialism and Foucault's dispositif—cuts anthropological inquiry loose from the exclusive focus on the figure of "the human" as well as from its exclusive attention to "human world-making."[47]

FIG. 3.3 Paul Klee, *Drüber und Empor*, 1931. Brush on paper on cardboard, 61.5 × 48.7 cm. This drawing nicely serves to illustrate the idea of an assemblage as a moving form, composed of different—and differently related—elements, each of which can itself be disassembled and recomposed. *Drüber und Empor. Above and Aloft.* Zentrum Paul Klee, Bern, Switzerland.

Three, the assemblage concept allows one to differentiate an anthropological, fieldwork-based inquiry into temporal difference from the mode of inquiry called history of science.

A study of conceptual movements in the here and now often relies on concepts derived from the history of science, most prominently "rupture" and "discontinuity."[48] While these concepts can no doubt be helpful, more often than not they are a burden to anthropologists for two reasons.

First, the historians of science who invented the concepts "rupture" and "discontinuity"—most famously Gaston Bachelard and Georges Canguilhem—were working on the past. That is, they already knew that the conceptual breaks they studied had accumulated—gradually or suddenly—into major events in the history of science (that is, for the most part, why they studied these breaks/ruptures). The anthropologist who works in the here and now doesn't have the comfort of hindsight. On the contrary, immersed in the chance encounters of fieldwork, there is no way for her to know whether the indices of movement (of change) she carefully captures in her notebooks are eventually going to be significant in a wider, more general sense.

Second, the concepts "rupture" and "discontinuity" were invented by historians and epistemologists to bring into view somewhat totalizing events: a rupture (or a discontinuity) serves to identify a breaking point that allows one to divide a story into a clear before and after. Again, the anthropologist of the here and now, working amid the chaos of fieldwork, can never quite know whether or not the changes (the movements) she seems to have found amount to a full scale rupture (or event).

If thinking in terms of assemblages—if relating to the present in terms of assemblages—is useful, it is not least because it allows to differentiate the study of movement from the study of ruptures (rupture—or discontinuity—is not the only form movement can take); it allows one to bring into analytical focus movements that unfold below the radar of those looking for ruptures—movements that can be interesting and curious for a whole variety of different reasons.

For example, a study of an assemblage might be less interested in a full-blown rupture than in the transfiguration of a single element of an assemblage and the almost undetectable changes in connections between elements that silently change what counts as true or that change the dynamic of a whole assemblage without an overt rupture ever occurring.[49]

Or such a study might be interested in decomposing a taken-for-granted truth in an assemblage that never stands still; it might be an effort to document the small lines of mutations that continuously but silently alter the elements of an assemblage that, on the surface of things, seems unchanging and stable. It might as well be an effort to detect how the arrival of a new element reconfigures the pattern of connectivity that seems to have governed an assemblage thus far.

Of course, a rupture (discontinuity) can still be the outcome of anthropological research—but for a study to be successful or interesting, it doesn't have to be.[50]

Take (one last example) the difference global health makes.

From the late 1940s to the late 1990s, world health was organized in the form of international health (IH). IH was grounded in the old eighteenth-century assumption that humanity comes in the form of a family of nations (each nations made up of one society, people, Volk), and that each nation has a government, which is responsible for the well-being of its society. Consequently, IH was composed of national populations, of national governments, and of international institutions, notably the WHO (and, since the 1970s, of emergency NGOs such as MSF).[51] For half a century, IH was a relatively stable assemblage (though arguably none of the defining elements ever stood still). In the late 1990s, however, a whole new set of institutions and actors dedicated to world health emerged and began to speak of global rather than international health: private foundations, philanthropies, NGOs, and private-public partnerships, many of which positioned themselves as alternatives to the WHO. Most famous among them are the Bill and Melinda Gates Foundation, Malaria no More, Label Red, the CUGH, the IHME, and the Clinton Foundation.[52]

Has the emergence of Global Health been a rupture? Is there a clear-cut distinction between a formation called GH and a formation called IH? Have the institutions constitutive of IH been rendered obsolete by the emergence of GH?

Hardly. The assemblage concept allows one to avoid the either/or logic of the rupture concept and to instead focus on how the emergence of new elements decentered elements that were formerly central (think of the effect of GH on the WHO) or how they reconfigured the connections between elements that defined what was possible and thereby gave rise to new venues of action (think of the emergence of private-public partnerships).[53]

not history

Isn't anthropology after ethnos a form of history, then? A history of the here and now?[54]

Precisely not.

A historian, by disciplinary default, will understand the present as a historical moment—even if the here and now is a moment of change, of turbulence. As history is for her the unfolding of time, and as nothing can exist outside of time, everything that is must be thought of as the product of history.

An anthropology after ethnos is not dismissive of history—and yet, it has radically broken with what one could call a historical mode of reasoning (which doesn't mean to say that it cannot make use of this mode).

How so?

Well, insofar as the aim of an anthropology after ethnos is to focus on that which escapes the already established—which escapes the possibilities implicit in the already thought and known—its focus is precisely not on history but on those aspects in the here and now that escape it, that cannot be explained by it.

Differently put, anthropology after ethnos is concerned with the unanticipated spaces of marvel and surprise that an incidental departure from the past opens up (and the reason it is unanticipated is precisely because it conceptually escapes the spaces of possibility that had historically structured the present up until now).

Take, for example, the idea of a "history of the present." Foucault's ambition, when he developed the history of the present, was to show how unlikely our contemporary categories of thought were until very recently, how much needed to happen to make them plausible, and, indeed possible. He was concerned with the present—he wanted to relieve the here and now of the already thought and known—but his intellectual tools where those of a historian: Foucault brought today into view as a product of yesterday.

To the anthropologists after ethnos, things look quite different: where Foucault writes the history of the present, the anthropologist after ethnos / interested in difference in time is interested in precisely those aspects of the here and now that escape the present of which Foucault has been writing the history. There is a vast gap, an abyss, between the field of history and the field explored by the anthropology after ethnos.

If one were to equate history with the timely, that is, with that which has existed in time, then the actual is not that which exists outside of time, as if it were an eternal realm, but the untimely. And this is precisely the challenge of the anthropology of the actual: to get at things untimely.

I cannot refrain from pointing out another powerful difference between the history of the present and the anthropology after ethnos: perhaps both seek, in their distinct ways, to liberate the present from the past. But can the historian of the present ever move beyond, well, the present? That is, can she ever depart from the categories of thought of which she writes the history? To ask the question is to answer it: the limit of the history of the present is that it remains part of the formation it problematizes.

Not so with the anthropology after ethnos: as a fieldwork-based mode of inquiry, it is focused on that which escapes the present understood as product of the past; it moves forward, it leaves behind, it explores new, unanticipated spaces of possibility that are still nascent, emergent, not yet—and perhaps never—stabilized.[55]

epochal (no more)

"You say you are interested in temporal differences. But if you sort time into a before and an after, then isn't it going to amount to a claim of epochal divides?"

The frequency with which I was asked this question, or some version thereof, has been a powerful reminder of just how sensitive anthropologists are to any interest in "difference in time."

How come?

On the one hand, there is the general implausibility of any sharp epochal ruptures—of the suggestion that clear-cut fault lines set apart conceptually coherent epochs from one another.

On the other hand—and for the discipline much more form giving—the reservation against epochal arguments is explained by the critique of the many ways in which anthropology has been contingent on and complicit with philosophies of history that have explained spatial differences (how people live elsewhere) in terms of a linear understanding of human history as progress (they still live in our past). The reference here is to Frantz Fanon (1961), Kathleen Gough (1967), Gerard Leclerc (1972), Talal Asad (1973), Bob Scholte ([1973] 1999), and Diane Lewis (1973); to Edward Said (1978), Johannes Fabian (1983) Fritz Kramer (1977), Dipesh Chakrabarty (2000), and Gayatri Spivak (1987, 1990). Through these critiques an acute political problematization of the articulation of any temporal differences has become a feature of anthropology.

What I have described as fieldwork-based anthropology after ethnos is deeply informed by both of these critiques.

First, if one thinks of the present in terms of assemblages—of contemporaneity—and if one thinks about change in terms of the nonlinear, multifaceted temporal movements (plural) of the various heterogeneous elements that make up any assemblage, then how could one maintain the illusion of the epochal? That is, the assumption that there are clear-cut ruptures that divide the world *au total* into a clear-cut before and after?

The mutations of the possible that an anthropology interested in temporal differences brings into focus have nothing of the grandeur of the epochal. No wave that washes away a face drawn in the sand at the edge of the sea—and then everything is different.

Second, at stake in a fieldwork-based anthropology after ethnos is hardly the establishment of a philosophy of history—neither in terms of the temporal mediation of spatial difference (the localization of people who live differently from us in our past) nor with respect to the consolidation of a unified schema of the history of humanity (from the state of nature to the present). What is at stake, instead, are instances of temporal difference that disrupt the conceptual presuppositions that have rendered possible given fields of knowledge—not least the field of history (or the history of humanity) itself.

Provocatively put, rather than establishing histories, the anthropology of temporal difference exposes and thereby undermines—as an end in itself—the very condition of possibility of any history. A bit as if the anthropology of temporal difference were a revolt against the conceptualization of temporal difference as history.

4

on the actual

(rather than the emergent)

> Philosophy always arrives too late. . . . As the *thought* of the world,
> philosophy appears only in the period after the actual. . . . When philosophy
> paints its grey in grey, then a configuration of life has grown old, and cannot be
> rejuvenated by this grey in grey, but only understood; the Owl of Minerva
> takes flight only as the dusk begins to fall.
>
> HEGEL, *Philosophy of Right*

ONE

Could one argue that, today, the limits of philosophy—its coming too late, its undifferentiated grey in grey—define the potential of anthropology? Precisely insofar as anthropology, or at least the anthropology after ethnos, understands itself as a study of—as the thought of—the colorful explosions of the actual?[1]

In closing, I want to address this question by offering a sketch, still tentative, of one particular variant of an anthropology after ethnos—the anthropology of the actual.[2]

What, exactly, do I mean by "the actual"?

Perhaps the best way of taking up this question is to belittle it, to keep it small. At stake is no ontology (nor, as Hegel had it, a philosophy of history). Whether the actual exists or not, whether it is or isn't a reality sui generis, is of no relevance. At stake in my sketch is not a substantive argument about the world. At stake, rather, is the attempt to bring into view a particular kind of anthropological inquiry, one that isn't grounded in an effort to get at how things really are but rather in a particular way of relating to things in motion (in the register of the actual).[3]

I approach my challenge in the form of a theft: like a thief, I silently enter the work of a small set of authors and steal from them formulations—unrelated fragments of thought—that, if arranged in certain ways, allow me to bring into view what I mean by "the actual."[4]

What matters is neither hermeneutics nor disinterestedness. What matters, rather, is the subtle art of decontextualization and appropriation.

TWO

I begin with the writings of Michel Foucault (1926–1984).

In a late article, "Qu'est ce que les lumières?," Foucault notes that Immanuel Kant had a somewhat curious concept of the Enlightenment. To make his point, Foucault concentrates on an essay the German philosopher sent to the *Berlinische Monatsschrift*, a periodical that in 1784 had encouraged its readers to submit essays that would answer the question "Was ist Aufklärung?" In this essay, Foucault explains, Kant defined the Enlightenment as "neither a world era to which one belongs, nor an event whose signs are perceived, nor the dawning of an accomplishment." Instead the question—What is Enlightenment?— was taken up by Kant as a question of pure actuality: "La question," Foucault writes, "concerne la pure actualité."[5]

Though what does Foucault mean by "pure actuality"?

Kant, Foucault elaborates, was trying to understand the present in its own right and in its terms, that is, in its actuality. What this means, he goes on to say, is that Kant wasn't "seeking to understand the present on the basis of a totality or of a future achievement" (Foucault 1984, 34), as if they were part of a bigger whole of which it was unaware—or as if it were merely an instance on the way to a predefined future. Instead, Kant interpreted the present as an exit (*Ausgang*)—perhaps a better translation would have been "departure"—from everything that has been. Kant, Foucault writes, was "looking for a difference: the difference today makes with respect to yesterday" (34).[6]

For Foucault, then, the actual is the difference the present makes. To bring the actuality of the present into view, to show that and in what precise form it differed from the singular formation that reigned before, this was the challenge Foucault had set himself. At least that's what he said in 1984.

Foucault offers little more than a first, almost clumsy, and in any case insufficient sense of what "the actual" could mean. An opportunity to change this—to broaden and simultaneously refine the concept of the actual I seek to elaborate—I found in the writings of two authors who have never used the term in any conceptual way but in whose works one can hear resound, like one can hear an echo resound, Foucault's notion of a pure actuality: Gaston Bachelard (1884–1962) and Georges Canguilhem (1904–1995).

What if one exposes Foucault's notion of the actual in the works of Bachelard and Canguilhem?

A central theme of Bachelard's work was what he referred to as the "epistemological rupture" that set apart everyday conceptions of the real from the scientifically real.[7]

Up until the early twentieth century, Bachelard argued—in well over twenty books—that the real was either understood as constructed (Bachelard called this school of thought "idealism") or as ("materialism"). However, in the early twentieth century, specifically with Einstein's sketch of the theory of relativity in 1905 and the subsequent formulation of quantum physics, a conception of the real emerged that radically escaped the two established philosophical understandings of the real. Quantum physics, according to Bachelard, produced knowledge not of things as they exist in nature (he spoke of a "continuity of substance") but of things that were constituted by thought and made material by experiments (his favorite example of what he called "reified theorems" were isotopes produced by the cyclotron and then identified by mass spectrometry). In his words: "The trajectories which allow us to separate the isotopes in the mass spectrometer don't exist in nature; one has to produce them technically. They are reified theorems."[8]

If Bachelard repeatedly stressed that the knowledge of quantum mechanics defied both materialism (primacy of matter) and idealism (primacy of ideas), that was because he was adamant that the history of science was a kind of philosophical effort to document the formation and contemporary state of the human mind: Bachelard considered it his task to ceaselessly map shifts and discontinuities in the conceptual and experimental constitution of the real. This task implied the challenge of rendering visible how the new outgrew the already established and thereby opened up a need for new concepts and modes of understanding.[9]

Canguilhem, concerned with biology rather than with physics, radicalized and multiplied Bachelard's rupture concept. Where Bachelard was ultimately concerned with one rupture only—the rupture provoked by the new scientific spirit—Canguilhem argued that discontinuity was a general feature of the growth of biological knowledge.

Progress, for Canguilhem, was possible. However, progress was not a linear process, "a mere increase in volume, achieved by adding new insights to the already known." Instead, progress came in the form of epistemological ruptures. A new knowledge, according to Canguilhem, is new precisely insofar as it is conceptually incommensurable with the logical coherence that organized previous knowledges. Thus the new will inevitably undermine a taken-for-granted-truth, will transform it into a relic of a time when we did not yet know.[10]

Consequently, Canguilhem regarded the history of knowledge as one of fractures, of new beginnings, of novel entry points, each of which was a radical cut, introducing a sharp incommensurability that equaled the emergence of a new, hitherto unknown constitution of one region—or domain—of reality.

He found himself most intrigued, he wrote (2005, 53), with "times in which scientific progress is exploding, blasting traditional epistemology."[11]

What is the effect of the work of Bachelard and Canguilhem on our concept of the actual?

If looked at from the perspective of the two historians of science, it appears that Foucault's notion of a pure actual retained a sense of epoch. Even though Foucault departed from the philosophy of history, the differences he brought into view—he spoke of modernity, of reason, of Man—were of a rather grand scale and had a rather longue durée: Foucault was concerned with Western reality as such—and his "actual" was a somewhat coherent temporal period (modernity) that came into existence in the form of an epistemic event/rupture between 1780 and 1800 and unfolded, if in complicated ways, up until his time.

Almost the inverse is the case for Canguilhem. Not that he—or Bachelard—wasn't concerned with Western reality. However, the ruptures Canguilhem or Bachelard brought into view were of a smaller scale and more region-specific. What was breaking open was not a new period of the Western world, the advent of a new configuration of reality, but rather a fracture in one or several categories of knowledge constitutive of a particular domain of the real.

At stake is no longer one grand rupture occurring at the end of the classical age, the detonation waves of which we still can feel, waves that gave form to our bodies and the categories of our minds (or to the very concepts of body and mind). At stake, rather, is a multitude of regional fissures and fractions.[12]

Canguilhem and Bachelard, then, regionalize reality and thereby multiply the ruptures—the events.

A consequence of this regionalization and multiplication is that the actual no longer exists in the singular but in the plural. It still refers to the breaking open of what was—but this "open" now no longer refers to the difference a somewhat coherent temporal period makes; rather, it refers to the multiple regional instances of the breaking open of the real, the blasting open of novel spaces, past and present, each one an elsewhere or elsewise, escaping established ways of thinking and knowing, and constituting new ones.

FOUR

I embark on the last chapter of my nonlinear theft tour as I turn, with the help of Canguilhem, to Henri Bergson (1859–1941) and Gilles Deleuze (1925–1995).

Perhaps the most powerful way of circumscribing the notion of fractures Canguilhem has offered was his scathing critique of the search for precursors. "The inclination to search for precursors, to find and celebrate them," he remarked in a talk to fellow historians of science (2005, 34), "is a sure indicator of the incapacity of an epistemological critique." It is a sign of incapacity precisely insofar as the possibility of looking for a precursor—that is, for someone who already knew what we only know now—was apparently dependent on the current state of knowledge of a given field. At a previous time, when other truths reigned, one would have written a different history, would have assembled a different line of precursors. Hence, the task of the epistemologist was not to look for precursors—because there are no precursors—but to document how a new discovery, that is, the emergence of a new truth, inevitably amounted to a rupture with the established understanding and arrangement of the past.

Canguilhem's critique of the precursor is reminiscent of Henri Bergson's critique of the concept of "the possible."

Most philosophers assume, wrote Bergson (1946, 25), "that . . . the possibility of things predates their coming into existence," as if "the possible were present throughout, waiting, like a ghost, for the hour of its appearance."

According to Bergson, this was naïve. It was naïve, first, because it missed the factual, the continuous emergence of the genuinely new, that is, of the phenomena that undermine and escape what was, at a given time, considered "possible." It was naïve, as well, because it missed the fact that "our ordinary logic is a retrospective logic; it cannot help but project the presently real, reduced to possibilities, into the past" (Bergson 1946, 26).

The reason I turn to Bergson here is that, in sharp contrast to the epistemologists, his critique of the possible did not lead him to a philosophy of ruptures (as if one formation of the possible would be replaced by another, differently structured one). He was not unsympathetic to Bachelard's work—they were contemporaries—and yet he ultimately viewed his epistemology as a half movement in thought: it is not "the fixed placed side by side with the fixed . . . that is real," he wrote in a passage that reads as if directed toward Bachelard, "on the contrary, it is the flux, the continuity of transition, it is change itself that is real" (1946, 15).

For Bergson, the epistemologists focused too narrowly on the emergence of new formations. All they cared about was the succession of logically incommensurable epistemological units. They could go back and forth between them, could explore and explain their incommensurability—but they had never managed to discover that these formations were not formations but rather snapshots of ongoing, ceaseless movement. For Bergson, theirs was a staccato philosophy of movement. Though he aimed for more: couldn't one think of movement as such? Movement rather than ruptures?

I abandon Bergson here—his ultimately ontologizing effort to think of movement as the real is of no relevance for my endeavor—and instead turn to Deleuze, who has taken up Bergson's critique of the possible, without following the philosophy of the élan vital.

It is telling, for example, that where Bergson contrasted the possible with "the real," Deleuze dropped the real and instead contrasted the possible with—the actual. In many of his writings Deleuze explained with vehemence that he doesn't care much about philosophers who are interested in the possible, meaning that the possible is already inherent in things as they are, that he rather is interested in those who contemplate the "actual," a term that he used to refer to the open—the movement—that becomes visible when an old possible is set in motion, when a new, unanticipated possibility emerges.[13]

Deleuze, contrary to Bergson, did not try to think of movement—the actual—in the abstract. Rather, he was a philosopher of the concrete—the actual cannot be found independent of those situations in which a concrete formation is breaking open, in which the elements constitutive of a possible are entering a period of movement.

The task of the philosopher, for Deleuze (and for Félix Guattari) was to capture something of this movement, and to render it visible even in a stable, on-the-surface-of-things unmoving formation. The challenge was to capture something of the actual.

Bergson and Deleuze allow me to modify the concept of the actual in an important way. For Foucault—and through him, for Canguilhem and Bachelard—the actual came into view as the difference a new formation has introduced vis-à-vis an older one. The actuality of a new formation consisted in its logical—or epistemic—incommensurability with the previous formations, in its breaking open a new space of thought.

After Deleuze (and with Bergson and Guattari), the actual still refers to ruptures/events—but these ruptures/events are now decoupled from the rise of a successor formation. In fact, the event is no longer the falling apart of a formation itself, nor is it the emergence of some new formation, but rather it is the becoming visible of a radical openness, a radical sense of movement that reigns, perhaps only briefly, when what has seemed possible is undermined, when the world as we knew it breaks open and nothing new yet appears in the place of the old.

Call it irreducible openness. Call it ceaseless, inexhaustible movement. Call it, with Guattari and Deleuze (1994, 5), the "always new."

FIVE

And anthropology?

An anthropology of the actual would be a mode of inquiry grounded in the effort to capture instances of—the actual. It would conduct fieldwork—would immerse itself in the world—to find out if (some of) the categories that order our knowledge, that are constitutive of the human and the nonhuman as we know it, are breaking open, with the effect that the human and/or the nonhuman lose their coherence. And it would describe such fieldwork-based instances—such episodes—for the sole purpose of capturing something of the indeterminable movement that reigns in such moments of irreducible openness.

The challenge of conceiving of such an inquiry into the actual is to come up with an altogether different kind of anthropology, an anthropology that is not—strictly speaking—concerned with the production of knowledge (be it ethical or existential). Nor with concept work. Not that the anthropology of the actual shies away from knowledge (or from concept work). It doesn't. In fact, it is very much concerned with knowledge—with the possibility of knowledge and how these possibilities change, mutate, get reconfigured, or get dissolved. But precisely insofar as the anthropologist of the actual would immerse herself in scenes of everyday life to find instances of nonteleological movement—

of change, mutation, reconfiguration, dissolution—the knowledge it produces does not itself refer to any stable, object-like formation out there that could be known.[14] Rather, its knowledge comes in the form of recognitions, of openings, of surprises, of discoveries, of derailments.[15]

Its objects of analysis are instances in which objects dissolve (or mutate).

———

The anthropologist of the actual is not interested in discovering things as they really are (or as they are elsewhere). Instead she conducts fieldwork to discover instances in which the assemblages that have been unwittingly constitutive of things are suddenly exposed and fall apart into the bits and pieces out of which they had once been assembled.

Could one get a hold of these bits and pieces while they are in motion? Before they are reassembled in any (coherent) way?[16]

———

Likewise, the anthropology of the actual doesn't shy away from inventing concepts. But the concepts it invents are not the generalizations on which others could then build their research, which they could develop further, so that gradually a conceptual foundation for scientific investigation would be provided. Rather, its concepts are meant to capture something of that which escapes.

Its concepts aspire to be—quoting Guattari and Deleuze's felicitous phrase again—"always new."

A negative way of interpreting the kind of anthropological endeavor I sought to outline here is to call it a limit approach: it exposes its concepts of knowledge, of thought, of living in order to indicate their limits.

A positive way of circumscribing the anthropology of the actual would be to say that fieldwork as exposure gives rise to observations—to anecdotes, observations, surprises, discoveries—that enable the researcher to move beyond the mapping of limits and antinomies and to capture the order of things themselves in motion, to capture movement, the play of movement at work.[17]

———

An observation.

The actual is a *plurale tantum*; it comes in many forms, none of which is reducible to any other one. The actual, like movement—or the open—does not exist in the abstract, independent of what is moved. It is a relational, not an ontological, mode (functional, not substantive). Consequently, *the* actual—as if it were some universal realm behind or inbetween things—does not exist. Every claim in that direction would be a time-and-place-specific abstraction that would sooner or later be set in motion.

Hence, my description of the anthropology of the actual as a relational mode of inquiry.[18]

SIX

In its focus on the nonteleological, the anthropology of the actual radically differs from the broad formation of the anthropology of the emergent. Both kinds of projects—the study of the actual and the study of the emergent—might focus on scenes of conceptual turbulence. However, they immerse themselves in these scenes to radically different (though not necessarily incommensurable, potentially even complimentary) ends.

———

In a way, the actual is implicit in the emergent—but the emergent is incommensurable with the actual.

———

Those interested in the emergent are intrigued by the gradual (or sudden) emergence of a successor formation. In sharp contrast, the anthropologist of the actual is indifferent to the emergence of a new stable form, whether one calls this new form a "dispositif" or an "apparatus," whether one speaks about infrastructure or the construction of new technical systems or the rise of a novel actor-network or—I could go on.

It is not that these approaches would not be interesting. And yet, for those who care about the actual, all these approaches have one flaw—their research is (however implicitly) teleologically structured. The anthropologists of the emergent conduct research in order to identify the final formation that will eventually—emerge. Thus, they are (remain) blind to movement as such, to nonteleological movements that reign when old concepts no longer work, that render words and things instable. For all those interested in successor formations, movement itself, movement as such, movement for movement's sake does not matter. It is mere noise one can ignore.

But what if the goal were to capture movement as such? Movement for movement's sake?

A sensibility for the actual opens up an analytical space—and project—where those interested in the emergent see and find nothing. Or, to be more precise, analytical spaces and projects, in the plural.

Thus the task of the anthropologist of the actual is not to get a hold of the coming into existence of a new formation, call it the putting in place of a new possible (of new concepts, of new categories of knowledge and thought, new orders of words, things, and the human)—but rather to capture something of the open that reigns when an old formation crumbles, to capture movement as such (as an end in itself) or, differently put, words and things that are *émouvé*.

One could increase the distance between the actual and the emergent even further.

Isn't it precisely one of the most powerful findings of the anthropology of the actual that, at least to date, no concept, no category, was ever standing still? Isn't it one of its major observations that movements—noise—occur not only when an old possible breaks open? That even a given possible is, underneath the surface, moved? And isn't it precisely one of the aims of the anthropology of the actual to render visible such movements in the apparently unmoved? The untimely in the timely?

From the perspective of the anthropology of the actual, then, the interest in the emergent is (potentially) caught in an eternal structure-antistructure-structure schema that can give rise only to a chronicle of successor formations. It is a residue of the epochal and thus, ultimately, of a linear philosophy of history.[19]

SEVEN

What effect does a sensibility for the actual have on the anthropologist?

The question may seem odd and yet, the practice of attending to the actual has powerful consequences.

For example, from the perspective of the actual each and any concept, each and any category, comes into view as fragile—as potentially but a fleeting, temporary formation, the product of a regional history of thinking and knowing that is constitutive of the things it thinks and knows, a history that will sooner or later fail in the face of this or of that event.

The consequence is that the anthropologist of the actual cannot—though let me say that no one ought to be reducible to one kind of anthropology only, actual or otherwise—engage in the production of knowledge that naively mistakes the things constituted by one's intellectual presuppositions for things objectively existing out there. From the perspective of the actual, the things "out there" are not really things out there but constitutions made possible by an order of thought, and with each mutation of this order of thought the things it made possible will mutate as well.

These things include the human thing.

Likewise, the anthropologist of the actual cannot—no longer—participate in the effort to foster general analytical concepts that would then, once and for all, guide inquiry and eventually allow building the house of truth.

Culture (or the cultural), subjectivity (or the subject), society (or the social)—these are not facts about but (contingent) constitutions of the human. There is nothing obvious about these concepts, nothing necessary. There have been different ones before, and it is likely that others will follow.

The anthropologist of the actual can no longer naively work with them, as if they were a given. She cannot, because for her, the critical distance opened up by the actual—the space of the untimely in the timely—has become the condition of the possibility of genuine anthropological work, that is, of the work of thought on thought, conducted—by way of fieldwork/research—in order to find instances of the breaking open of the established, in order to capture something of the movements constitutive of this openness.

She has become blasé by timeless concepts. She has become blasé—one grand ennui—by concepts that are blind to their own timeliness.

Governmentality, biopolitics, subjectivity, life itself, technologies of the self, the social, apparatuses, the body, nature or nature cultures, bare life, suffering, flexibility, *homo sacer*, neoliberalism, people—I could go on.

She cannot help but look at these concepts as opportunities to provoke—as invitations to tease, to wonder out loud, to undermine, to conduct research to find and render visible the actual, that is, that which upsets these concepts, and renders them, ultimately, useless.

———

And politics?

For the anthropologist of the actual every political program (just like every moral doctrine and every theory of knowledge) will lose the givenness it has for those who commit to it. Her activism is not timely—but untimely. The way forward, for her, is to withdraw from participating in these programs and to instead map the contingencies that gave rise to them, the events, surprises, and discoveries that escape them and set them in motion, and will eventually undermine them. The way forward, for her, is to find movement, to be found by it, to release it, to set in motion.

Could one call this kind of anthropological inquiry political?[20]

Provocation is a side effect of the joy of liberation the anthropology of the actual amounts to. A provocation to all those who practice the human sciences (anthropology) in the name of the irrefutable, of knowledge, of certainty, of the breakthrough to the truth.

the new/different
(of movement/in terms of movement)

Throughout this book, or so I recognize in retrospect, I wrote of the new or of the new/different.

Why?

One of the many reasons for writing this book has been my curiosity to see if I couldn't cut loose "the new" from any linear comprehensions of time.

It was my ambition to decouple the new/different from the epochal and thus from linear philosophies of history (and progress). I wanted to provincialize (and pluralize) the new (make it domain specific), to set the study of the new apart from the study of history (or historical progress), and to differentiate the actual from the emergent (to desubstantiate the new into the actual).

What is more, I wanted to elaborate the possibility of a radical new, that is, a new understood as the unanticipated breaking open—suddenly or slowly—of a space of thought, of a possibility of being in the world that escapes the already known, a possibility so radically different—new—that no one could plan or foresee its emergence.

I wanted to construct a conception of the new that would defy all efforts to scale it up, to capitalize on it, to colonize it, to know it.

I wanted to allow for the emergence of a concept of the new that would convey the sense that everything could be different.

And I wanted to elaborate a notion of the new that opens up the possibility of (ceaseless) escape.

What is the science adequate to the new/different, to escapes?

The answer I have tried out—with as much hesitation as excitement—has been "an analysis of movement/in terms of movement." The reason for this suggestion is that a form of research that puts at stake its own analytical concepts—the codings of the human and of the real they silently transport—in one's fieldwork, and that makes the derailment of just these concepts and codings the focus of its inquiry, is that it doesn't require to be ontologically grounded. On the contrary, it is grounded in the curiosity if that which is taken to be ontologically true is set in motion.

Differently put, it cares less about "the truth" than about the production, by way of exposure and escape, of a surplus of possibilities of truth—a surplus that no administrator of the already achieved and accomplished can ever exhaust.

why and to what ends (philosophy, politics, poetry)

"I very much like your insistence on an anthropology of the actual and the manner in which you spell out what it is not," a senior colleague wrote to me after she had read through the manuscript. "I also like how the actual is not, if handled appropriately, scalable, or open to colonization. One overriding concern I had though was what does one 'do' with the actual; the fissure?"

Indeed, why does one practice an anthropology of the actual? And to what ends?

Here is a list of seven efforts to engage these two questions. Some of my replies blur the line between the why and the how—but, you see, when it comes to practical matters, the why and the how are difficult to differentiate.

One

You ask me for the "why."

It is not that I don't understand or appreciate. Rather, it is that I wonder whether the why question can really be addressed to the anthropology of the actual. I would like to doubt it. I would like to doubt it, first, because the why question ultimately is a utility question. It wants to know "What is it good for?" In my understanding, however, the anthropology of the actual is a refusal to be useful—is an effort to render visible non-teleological movements that are irreducible to any form of utility. I would like to doubt it as well, second, because the why question implies that the anthropology of the actual would be a means toward an end, an end presumably outside of the stakes of the actual. But what if the anthropology of the actual had no ends outside itself? If it were self-sufficient? If there indeed were ends, if the anthropology of the actual were a mere tool, then wouldn't this imply that there are constants? And wouldn't that imply reinserting the actual—the irreducibly different—into a horizon organized by the already known? For surely, the end must predate one's inquiry, an inquiry conducted to achieve an end. No, the anthropology of the actually cannot be a mere tool—or it ceases being an anthropology "of the actual."

The actual—or the anthropology thereof—cannot be instrumentalized.[21]

Two

I think of the anthropology of the actual as a practice of curiosity—if of a peculiar kind of curiosity. If curiosity is usually assumed to be an expression of the will to know, then the curiosity constitutive of the anthropology of the actual isn't concerned with knowledge at all. It doesn't ask in order to find out. Rather, it is content with asking. Indeed, it is a curiosity that is not interested in answers at all but rather in questions, in the production of a surplus of questions no one can exhaust; it is a boundless, ceaseless curiosity directed at everything, including itself.

Three

The third entry in my list of replies describes the anthropology of the actual as a philosophical exercise (p, not P; thought concrete, not abstract). An exercise that consists in tracing how accidents—or the unanticipated, the unexpected, the unforeseen—set in motion (some of) the philosophical presuppositions that have silently (unnoticeably) constituted the real, with the consequence that what the real is changes. The goal of these philosophical exercises (plural), however, is not to determine what the new, emergent configuration of the real is—but rather to capture what one could call "pure becoming," that is, becoming as such, becoming that is not yet on its way to becoming some "thing."

(I add that it seems to me untenable—and ultimately self-deceptive—to assume one could exempt one's own analytical vocabularies from the actual.)

Four

The anthropology of the actual is an ethical practice.

How shall I live? What can I do?

Imagine the human were a space of possibilities—a space defined by possible relations, to oneself and others—constituted and stabilized by philosophical presuppositions inscribed in and transported by concepts, practices, and infrastructures that often (but not necessarily) lie far away from the human. Couldn't one say then that each time the unexpected sets in motion one or several of these presuppositions, the space of possibilities constitutive of the human is set in motion as well? With the consequence that who or what one is or can be is changing?

Five

As I see it, the anthropology of the actual is a form of politics. Indeed, attending to the actual is for me a radical political practice, a practice of freedom (of escape). My reference here is foremost to Michel Foucault. With Foucault, I am concerned with how to expose and escape power/knowledge—that is, instances in which (not only) humans are subjected to a knowledge that is seemingly uncontroversial but that is, like all knowledge, contingent and hence inherently instable. This is why I stress the nonteleological, "the always new" (Deleuze and Guattari), the irreducibly different.

There is this aberrant idea in the human sciences that only the knowledge of the natural sciences—or of governments, philanthropies, NGOs, administrators—makes for power/knowledge. I consider this absurd. The categories of critique—political or moral—are by no means external to the actual, on the contrary. The challenge thus becomes how to articulate critique while not excluding the terms—the conditions of possibility—constitutive of critique.

Six

I think of the anthropology of the actual as fundamentally a practice of poetry. If not in terms of form then at least in terms of the sensibilities its object demands: the challenge is to attend to that which undermines utility and defies ends—call it the irreducibly different, ceaseless movement, the nonteleological, that which escapes (I say "if not in its form" because I do not want to exclude the possibility of writing about the actual in iambic pentameter, classical hexameter, or the free use of lines).

The anthropology of the actual is concerned not with the prose of the world but with its poetry—and its poetic aim is to render visible instances of the invisible.[22]

Seven

The last but by far the most important entry in my list of responses is joy.

To immerse oneself in the concrete, to attend to the actual, to find (and make use of) lines of escape—gives rise to an intense feeling of joy, a feeling that is increased if it is shared with friends.[23]

coda

(a dictionary of anthropological commonplaces)

ONE

When I first began thinking about writing this book, I developed the habit of collecting sentences that seemed indebted to the conception of "the human" that emerged in the late eighteenth century. The background to this venture off into the world of collectors was a curio j5sity I had harbored for a long time.

What actually holds the vastly diverse fields ploughed by anthropologists together as "anthropological"? Was there perhaps a small set of conceptual presuppositions about "the human" that organized the vast majority of studies independent of their actual field? Could I draw up a list of these "scripts"?

Think of it as part of my strategy for finding possibilities of "escape."

For a long time—years—I was reading anthropology books of different ages, concerned with wildly different things, from meaning construction in rituals to design, from city planning to social suffering. And as I read, I found myself increasingly struck by how little variation there seemed to be: anthropology seemed to me to be one big conceptual machine in which one could feed pretty much anything and in the end it would always print a similar picture of "the human."

I could not help but think of my list of scripts—with reference to Gustave Flaubert (1821–1880)—as a dictionary of exhausted, long-worn-out anthropological commonplaces.

What intrigued me about this association was not the bored arrogance with which Flaubert turned to his contemporaries. To the French author, his dictionary was not just a collection of platitudes, of empty, long-anachronistic wisdom that somehow maintains the illusion of significance. First and foremost, it was a document of general human stupidity. Flaubert used the dictionary as an opportunity to elevate himself above this stupidity. I have no interest in such self-elevation—none. As anyone who reads a single line of my work can tell, my work is by no means free of commonplaces (indeed, I don't know how to leave commonplaces—or scripts—fully behind). And second, not a single study I read was reducible to what the French author called *le grand ennui*.

If, despite my critique of Flaubert, I found it useful to draw a parallel between my list of anthropological commonplaces and Flaubert's dictionary, it was only insofar as it allowed me to make visible what increasingly seemed to me a problem: the disarming poverty of the epistemic figure of "the human" on which anthropologists, including myself, have been relying for so long.

Differently put, Flaubert provided the possibility to bring into view what I still think of as the poetic and political challenge of breaking—by way of fieldwork/research—with the scripts that have structured anthropological research.

The ambition would be to break the scripts that structured research by way of exposing them in one's fieldwork—by way of creating the condition for the possibility of derailment (research as exposure).

I admit that, on a bad day, I easily could get frustrated by the repetition of assertions I had already read a thousand times (in my own work as well as in the work of others). Some of my notes lament that anthropologists seem unaware of their own condition of possibility, a condition deeply provincial and thoroughly problematic. To make things worse, many authors seemed to take for granted "the human" as the irrefutable truth that must be defended if human dignity is to be maintained.

But then, all too often my sense of despair was simply a reflection of the predicaments I ran into in my efforts to find ways to cut loose anthropology from "the human."

Though on good days I was overflowing with excitement.

It was because of this mixture of despair and excitement that I decided to write a chapter—chapter 2—that exposes the historicity of this figure of the human. And it is partly because of this sense of despair that I decided to publish a short selection from my dictionary.

Think of it as one last (one more) act of provocation: as my effort to enroll you in my restless search for escapes.

TWO

To allow for a sense of anonymity, I replace mentionings of places with PTIS (*the place that I study*) and references to things studied with TTIS (*the thing that I study*).

"In this book I show that the TTIS is culturally constituted."

"All of this amounts to saying that the disease I study is really a cultural category."

"The effects of TTIS on society are far from settled."

"This book asks *Is society investing in the right things?*"

"Society is obsessed with the TTIS."

"I study the effect of the TTIS on society."

"We need to pay attention to the unknown consequences of the TTIS on society."

"Humans are social beings, live in societies."

"This book shows that science not only produces particular types of knowledge . . . but also leads to normative and politically charged ways of intervening."

"I study how the TTIS changes everyday notions of biological and social life."

"Social scientists should attend to the norms, values, and politics that are wrapped up within the TTIS."

"I argue that translational challenges are not only technical but also social, involving negotiations about meaning, form, and value."

"I argue that personalized medicine is deeply intertwined with techniques of knowledge and power."

"This is a book about the TTIS. More specifically, this book is an ethnographic study of the TTIS in the PTIS."

"I analyze how the TTIS works in the PTIS. I focus on everyday life and show the TTIS acquires a certain political meaning."

"The aim here is to politicize the everyday world."

"Although seemingly neutral, a careful and critical study of the TTIS shows that it unwittingly reproduces inequalities."

"What I present in this book, then, is an ethnography of the premise that in the PTIS the TTIS is political in a way that is particular to the PTIS. My argument here is that TTIS is a cultural theorem for explaining relations between people, things, and politics in the PTIS."

"In this book I ask *How are things made to mean?*"

"Furthermore, I ask how meaning construction helps shape the social world."

"What most prior books on the TTIS have passed over too quickly is the nature of the TTIS as a cultural phenomenon, as assemblage of actors, practices, forms, and ideologies that all sit at the very core of what Nelson Goodman calls ways of world making."

"In most instances the TTIS is a locally contingent and culturally elaborated process of production, a background scheme organizing the ways in which things are made."

"What we need now is a critical anthropology of the TTIS, that is, ethnographic projects that articulate the cultural imaginaries and micropolitics that delineate the TTIS's promises and practices."

"What we need to study is the ongoing production and reproduction of social worlds."

"This transformation . . . is far from neutral. It has produced a culture of fresh social inequalities."

"I bypass the field of reason and seek to open an understanding of the human in terms of affect."

"This book is an ethnographic examination of the ways in which the TTIS, in the PTIS, generates and relies upon inequalities, even as it strives to end them."

"A central aim of this book is to interrogate the practices and politics of the TTIS through an exploration of the interplay between science, technology, and inequality."

"I argue against the idea that disease is a freestanding biological phenomenon that exists separately from the social world."

"I reject the notion of science as autonomous from social relations."

"I insist on rigorous social contextualization of entities that are often taken for granted as objective, natural phenomena."

"At stake in the TTIS is biopower—the control of bodies and populations through forms of management and administration."

"Even benevolent efforts to govern or improve social welfare must be theorized as forms of symbolic violence or therapeutic domination aimed at cultivating docile, self-disciplined bodies."

"What is at stake in my anthropology is primarily a concern with the politics of suffering and inequality."

"Human suffering and scientific knowledge have over the past three decades been deeply interdependent."

"By focusing on the sociotechnical construction of bodies and maladies, anthropologists are raising crucial questions about the practice of science in an unequal world."

"Anthropology is increasingly interested in questions of power and knowledge production."

"Human nature is fundamentally political."

one last question

"One last question," she says. "Why, given that you break with the human, do you continue to speak of anthropology? I mean, why speaking of anthropology at all?"

I had found myself confronted with the question several times before. Most often it had been posed in somewhat legal—in disciplinary—terms. A bit as if I needed to be reminded that what I described as anthropology had little to do with the discipline of anthropology and that, besides, there was no obvious reason for the discipline to accommodate the project I was outlining. Why, thus, would I speak of anthropology? Was I entitled to use the phrase?

"I am not sure what the stakes of the question are," I begin a hesitant reply, "but very generally speaking, I speak of anthropology not for disciplinary reasons but simply and perhaps naively because I am interested in things human, in how the human is, at different times, in different scenes, constituted, in how spaces of possibility within which we comprehend ourselves, in how the terms we have available to think about ourselves, are mutating over time. This is to say, my goal has not at all been to reject a curiosity about things human. What interests me is the possibility of decoupling this curiosity about things human from 'the human,' from the conceptualization of humans in terms of 'Man,' from the comprehension of the world that this comprehension transports."

"I understand that," she says. "And I don't care about the disciplinary all that much. Though maybe we should?"

"Maybe it is where we are coming from. Obviously my writing is inflected by my training, for better or worse. But I also think of the kinds of questions I cannot help but wonder about as, well, postdisciplinary."

"Anyhow, what concerns me is that your response sounds too facile. It conceals what seems to me to be at stake. It is not just that you let go of 'the human' or of 'Man.' You also want to let go of the idea that there is a distinctive human realm, or aspect of reality, no? And that is why I wonder if it makes sense for you to speak of anthropology at all?"

"But this idea of a separate, unique human realm, this is inseparably related to the effort to articulate 'the human,' no? I mean, it was only with the effort to articulate a general, time-and-place-independent concept of the human that the idea of a unique human realm emerged and that this idea got consolidated. Why begin one's anthropological research with wild ontological claims about what the human is even though we know about the historicity and contingency of these claims? Why would one take these claims as a foundation? Wouldn't that be a form of self-deception?"

"Let me ask with more precision. In my reading, you set out to break with the very certainty on which anthropology is built: that sometime in the eighteenth century we discovered that behind all the diverse life forms stands 'the human.' You undermine that certainty—and thus the legitimacy of anthropology—but you continue to talk about anthropology as if there were no problems at all. And that needs to be clarified."

"You say 'certainty,' but it is not certainty at all. I mean, not at all. Now, you may say, well, what is certain? And my response would be, well, then let's think about what happens when one lets go of certainty? Could one ground anthropology—not the discipline but the curiosity—in uncertainty? That is exactly what interests me."

"Ignorance."

"The appreciation of ignorance is a starting point. As a matter of honesty, as an epistemic virtue. This is also what I hold against ontology. The reason I don't want to begin with 'the human,' or why I don't want to ground anthropology in the idea that there is a separate, a distinct human reality that requires its own discipline—anthropology—is not that I want to problematize the human in the name of some bigger whole that we forgot, some bigger whole of which humans in reality are part and from the perspective of which one has to think of the human. Say, nature or the cosmos. That would simply mean to replace one self-deceptive certainty with another one. No, the reason I don't want to start with 'the human' is that I want to ground my research not in an answer—but in a question, in boundless questions. In a way, this is the theme of *After Ethnos*, even though I could not have articulated it this way when I set out to write it: Is it possible to come up with a sketch, however modest and tentative, of an anthropology that is devoid of ontological groundings? Devoid of a substantive concept of the human (this is human reality, this is how it is composed, this is how it needs to be studied), devoid of ontological conceptions of the world (this is how the world is structured, and this is the place of the human in the world), devoid as well of an anthropocentric epistemology that grounds everything in the human? And the by and large heuristic key terms of what my sketch of a non-ontology-based anthropology is are "exposure," "the new/different," "escape," "mutation," "thinking about thinking," "analysis of movement in terms of movement," and "the actual."

"I would say that anthropology, the formation from which you break away, was not devoid of curiosity. But from the perspective you open up, I guess its own condition of possibility—what I called its certainty—was exempted from this curiosity."

"That is how I see it, I think. And I would say that beginning with ignorance allows curiosity to expose the taken for granted in particular. In a way, what I am interested in is the possibility of a science of things human that revolves around surprise, around the unexpected. And what I mean by 'surprise' or 'the unexpected' are findings that emerge from research as exposure that cannot be explained in terms that we have thus far relied on when speaking about the human. Almost inevitably, then, these findings are going to make visible something thus far taken to be true about humans as a presupposition. So that an answer is mutated into a question."

"But you see that what you describe under the term 'anthropology' is very different from how anthropology has been understood? In fact, it runs diagonal to it."

"Because it refuses to ground anthropology in a substantive concept of the human?"

"And, in a way, because it has no real ontological ambitions."

"It has no ontological ambitions because it revolves around exposure or the unknown rather than around the effort to stabilize the already known. It cannot help but distrust any ontology."

She nods.

"How would you describe," I ask, "this radical curiosity about things human? I know of no better term for this curiosity than 'anthropology,' no?"

notes

ON ANTHROPOLOGY (FREE FROM ETHNOS)

1. My understanding of "classical modernity" is indebted to Peukert (1987) and Licht-blau (1996), who both give a brilliant portrayal of the philosophical-conceptual events that marked—and unsettled—the period between roughly the 1880s and the late 1920s.

2. The phrase "poetic and political" is a reference to the subtitle of Marcus and Clifford (1986).

3. The exemplary early reference here is to Dell Hymes's *Reinventing Anthropology* (Hymes 1974), originally published in 1972, with essays by, among others, Gerald Berreman, Eric Wolfe, Bob Scholte, and Laura Nader. On the pre-1970s critique, cf. especially Bunzl (2005).

4. The various critical and revisionist programs went off in different, partly incommensurable, directions and favored radically different visions of anthropology, of what it should be about, and of which political stance it should take. For a partial attempt to provide an over view see Rabinow et al. (2008).

5. Both classic modern ethnography and classic modern art (and also classic modern architecture) emerged in the late nineteenth century, reached a high point in the early decades of the twentieth century, and disappeared after WWII (while remaining a major reference until the 1970s).

6. For two excellent studies, see Michael Harbsmeier (1985) and Justin Stagl (1995).

7. See, for example, Kramer (1977) and Fabian (1983).

8. Exemplary efforts to introduce a historic dimension into ethnography were offered by Eric Wolf (1982), Renato Rosaldo (1980), and Richard Price (1983).
A major intellectual background to such historically informed ethnographies has been Marx's idea of "weltgeschichtliche Tatsachen." Wallerstein has translated this into a world system theory (Marcus 1986; Marcus and Fischer 1986). Today this is present not only in the idea of multiple modernities in postcolonial theory but also in the new genre of Weltgeschichte; cf. Bayly (2003) and Osterhammel (2009).

9. Cf., for example, (Tedlock 1979, Crapanzano 1980, Dwyer 1982, Rosaldo 1980, Marcus and Clifford 1986, Clifford 1989). I would also like to mention here the seminal Tsing (1993).
The "experimental" refers here to Marcus and Fischer (1986).

10. Marcus and Clifford (1986, 241). Of course, anthropologists worked "at home" before. One thinks, for example, of Warner (1949a, 1949b), Warner and Lunt (1941), Warner and Low (1947), Warner and Henry (1948). But these anthropologists at home worked under the classical paradigm, with the analytical tools of the discipline, even where they adapted them to local circumstances (Warner studied anthropology at Berkeley, under Lowie and Kroeber, got his anthropology PhD at Harvard, and was a Prof at Chicago, working alongside Radcliffe-Brown, to whom his work was thoroughly indebted). It did not lead to questioning the old and inventing a new toolkit. It did not lead, on the level of questions asked, to a conceptually or methodologically new or qualitatively different project.

11. For example, feminist ethnographers began to study the biomedical construction of women (Martin 1987, 1994; Rapp 1988, 1990) and the ways in which new reproductive technologies challenged established concepts of kinship and gender (Collier and Yanagisako 1987; Strathern 1988, 1991, 1992a, 1992b; Franklin 1997; Edwards et al. 1999; Weston 1991); critical medical anthropologists documented the significance of culture for understanding the biology of disease (Lock and Gordon 1988; Lock 1993; Kleinman 1988; Lin and Kleinman 1988) and pointed out silent correspondences between medicine and Western political hegemony (Scheper-Hughes 1992); and anthropologists of science documented how the seemingly universal is locally produced and inseparably entangled with broader political and economical developments (Gusterson 1996; Rabinow 1989, 1996a, 1999; Traweek 1988).

12. Today, this new kind of anthropology is often referred to as "the anthropology of the contemporary." The phrase "anthropology of the contemporary" was first introduced by Paul Rabinow in 1999 and has since been further elaborated by him, see Rabinow (2003, 2008).

13. See (Marcus 1995; Gupta and Ferguson 1997a, 1997b; M. Fischer 1999, 2004; Rabinow 2003; Bornerman 2007; Cerwonka and Malkki 2007; Rabinow et al. 2008).

14. See Rabinow et al. (2008) and the reviews thereof, e.g., (Salazar 2009, Formoso 2011, Foley 2011, Krauss 2011, Trujillo 2011, Poktonjak 2010). See as well the *Experimental Futures* book series at Duke edited by Joe Dumit and Michael Fischer and the very interesting article by Anand Pandian (2012), "The Time of Anthropology."

15. I am grateful to Fritz Kramer and Ronald Niezen for many clarifying conversations on this subject.

16. I write this in German here with reference to Immanuel Kant. On Kant's anthropology, see Foucault (2008a); on the context of Kant's question, see Brandt (2014) and Zammito (2002).

17. Brilliantly argued by David Schneider, whose "culturalization" of nature and society has later been taken up, on the one hand, by Collier and Yanagisako (1987) and, on the other, by Marilyn Strathern (1992a). Authors such as Stefan Helmreich (2003)—in conversation with the work of Donna Haraway (1991, 1997)—have developed this further.

18. The terms of analysis, from the cultural point of view, therefore, must be interpretative ones—either derived from philology or from semiotics, from hermeneutics or deconstructivism.

Let me add that, of course, social and cultural anthropology are not mutually exclusive. Meaning centered approaches may well be coupled with societal questions. And such a coupling has in fact often—and very productively—been achieved.

19. What has led to this problematization—to this departure from anthropology in its form of ethnography—has been the taking serious of an insight that as such perhaps isn't "new" but that gains "new" significance in the context of the conceptual reorientation characteristic of contemporary anthropology: that the discipline's established ways of posing and answering the question concerning the human—*Was ist der Mensch?*—are anything but evident. Universals, as Félix Guattari and Gilles Deleuze noted in 1994, don't explain anything, they need to be explained.

I regret that I cannot rehearse here the philosophically important efforts to question the centrality of "der Mensch" for philosophy. Most important references for me have been Hannah Arendt's *The Human Condition* (1958); Martin Heidegger's *Die Zeit des Weltbildes* ([1938] 1950) and his *Brief über den Humanismus* (1947); Michel Foucault's *Les mots et les choses* ([1966] 1990) and his *Introduction to Kant's Anthropology* (2008). In general one has to mention here the French critique of subject philosophy—the antihumanists as they were (wrongly so, I think) called—Lévi-Strauss, Lacan, Barthes, Foucault, Derrida, Deleuze, and Guattari.

20. For a related, complementary effort to differentiate anthropology from culture— or to imagine an anthropology after culture—see Lila Abu-Lughod's article "Writing Against Culture" (1991). The occasion for her essay was provided by the publication of *Writing Culture*. Infamously, the volume edited by Marcus and Clifford in 1986 had excluded feminist critiques. Abu-Lughod, pointing out that she writes from the perspective of "feminists and halfies," brilliantly showed that the culture concept inevitably relies on an essentialization of difference, a difference between self and other that is organized in terms of temporal distance and political asymmetry. The fact that *Writing Culture* excludes the perspective of feminists and halfies, she writes, allowed it to hold on to a politically and epistemologically problematic concept.

See as well Donna Haraway's critique of the culture concept in her "Cyborg Manifesto" ([1984] 1991) and Dipesh Chakrabarty (2000).

21. For anthropological thoughts on Avian Flu see Rees (2010a); Caduff (2010), Lowe (2012). For a philosophically inclined anthropology of the Internet, see especially Kelty (2009).

22. On yeast biology see Roosth (2009), on insects see Raffels (2011), on dogs see Haraway (2003, 2008), on Avian flu see footnote 21, on HIV see Biehl (2007), on adult neurogenesis see Rees (2010b, 2015c, 2016).

23. In this respect the philosophically inclined anthropology of the contemporary differs from the German tradition of philosophical anthropology. Where the latter looks to the sciences in order to answer the question of Man, in order to philosophically synthesize the answers science gives, so that a coherent comprehension of the human emerges, the latter looks to various sciences—and other fields—to see where new ways, implicit or explicit, of posing the question or of answering it emerge; the former is a question-based approach, the latter answer-based.

24. The reference here is to Michel Foucault (1985) *The Use of Pleasure*, vol. 2 of *The History of Sexuality*.

25. Of course, one may say that ethnography—where it was concerned with the native point of view rather than with society and culture—has always been a philosophical enterprise. That it has always undermined the self-evident, always opened up concrete new spaces of thought (see my interviews with Fritz Kramer in Kramer [2005]). I comply—but think (1) that the terms of possibility that have organized ethnography have become impossible to maintain. I think as well (2) that what I have called a philosophically inclined anthropology continuous to be informed—if in broken, never easy, always complicated and troubled ways—by the interest in differences on the level of thought that has been central to one line of classical modern ethnography: though where classical ethnographers have turned toward faraway life forms the anthropologist after ethnos studies what one may loosely call the emergent. The differences that come into view is less spatial than temporal (see chapter 2 of this book). Arguably, the reintegration of the spatial into the temporal is one—not the only one and perhaps not the central one—of the great challenges of the anthropology after ethnos: how to empirically travel the terrain of questions formerly left to classical ethnography after the end of classical ethnography? The best example I know is Kramer und Marx (1993).

To highlight the coming into existence of a philosophically inclined anthropology, then, is not so much an expression of disregard for the interest in spatial differences between life forms, in what has been called "the native point of view" (even though it grounds in a radical break with the presuppositions that have made this interest possible in the first place).

I am particularly grateful to Johannes Quack for many discussions of this question.

26. Let me add here that precisely insofar as it opens up a space beyond the answer-based anthropology of modern ethnography it is, despite the fact that it asks how humans are thought and known, not anthropocentric (in that it doesn't ground its inquiry in an anthropocentric epistemology; see chapter 2).

27. I am ashamed that I learned of Tim Ingold's thought-provoking effort to differentiate anthropology from ethnography only when my manuscript was already through the copy-editing state. My work would have been better—more refined—had I been familiar with Ingold's work when I began the writing process.

While our work differs significantly, there are interesting parallels.

As I understand it, Ingold doesn't attempt to cut loose—to free—anthropology from ethnos. His project isn't the exposure of the answers—culture, history, society—on which anthropology has relied on (and along with it the vast majority of the human sciences). Rather, Ingold refuses the reduction of anthropology to ethnography.

Ethnography, to Ingold (2016, 1), is a science and as such a knowledge or data producing project: It reduces the world in which we live and with which we are inseparably interwoven (Ingold 2011) to "data" to be collected, interpreted, "and fashioned into authoritative knowledge." Ethnography, as he sees it, is "compliant with the protocols of normal science."

If the practice of ethnography as science is problematic to Ingold (2014; 2016, 1) then because its effect is a "rupture," is a "division between the real world (…) and the world of theory," that is, the world as it is produced by science (note how this parallels Gaston

Bachelard's 1934 account of science—except that Bachelard celebrates the poetry of science).

Anthropology, on the other hand, is the study of the real world—and as such has the power to "heal the rupture" (ed.). Anthropologists, so Ingold (2016, 4), "should be leading a campaign against the very idea that the world presents itself to human science as a standing reverse of data for collection."

To me, Ingold's critique of "normal science" and the comprehension of the world it produces is reminiscent of Heidegger's account of the worlds in which we live. Heidegger, in part II of *Being and Time*, suggests that everyday human life is not comprehensible in terms of modern science. It is not comprehensible, in fact, as long as one thinks of humans as *subjects* and of things in the world as *objects*. Rather, we have to understand the everyday as an unfolding in which humans and things are seamlessly interwoven in forms of processes and or habits. Heidegger's term *Zeugs*—translated as Equipment—provides an example: an artisan doesn't think of a tool as tool he uses to achieve this or that end. Rather, the artisan finds himself integrated—in thought, action, being—together with his equipment, in an unfolding process.

The concept of the world that emerges from ethnography as science, Ingold seems to suggest, is destructive—because it is wrong. And anthropology, understood as curiosity of the conditions of human life in the world, has the power—and the obligation—to correct the error.

Despite the obvious differences that set apart Ingold's anthropology from the philosophically inclined anthropology after ethnos (after the human) that I have sought to render visible here, there are joyful parallels. For example, we share the insistence—the observation—that the real exceeds the concepts and theories and scripts we operate with: it escapes them, undermines them, breaks them open. And we both are busy attempting to outline a comprehension of anthropology as the fieldwork-based effort to attend to just these escapes. As Ingold (2016, 2) nicely puts it: Fieldwork "frees us from the limitations of standpoints or perspectives and causes us continually to question what previously we would have taken for granted."

I am over-joyed about Ingold's disregard for theory, about his refusal to practice anthropology as a script based study of authoritative knowledge (Rees 2016 is effectively an effort to render visible the poetics of science, see as well Manoukian 2017, http://somatosphere.net/2017/08/on-plastic-reason-by-tobias-rees.html, accessed on February 5, 2018). It is just that I am troubled by his "ontological commitment" (2016, 5) to "the world" as the really real. Anthropology, or so Ingold at times sounds, has figured it out: it has broken through to the truth and now has to act as the guardian of this truth—and as its defenders. He asks anthropologists to acknowledge "our debt to the world for what we are and what we know (2016, 5)."

I have no such ontological commitments. And I get suspicious wherever someone claims to speak in the name of truth, scientific or moral: My work is an effort to release the world—humans—from the already thought and known and I think it is important to refuse the effort to articulate what I have called the open in form of a theory or concept or account (neither being nor becoming): Each such account ultimately is a closure. A critical tool of the anthropology after ethnos thus is the ceaseless detection of that which escapes—even when it comes to accounts of the open. The effort is to reconstitute irreducible (human) uncertainty.

See as well Ingold (2017).

28. According to Durkheim and Mauss, primitive societies were, in their survival, contingent on extreme social adhesion, on the valuation of the society over any individual interest—and such adhesion was greatly facilitated by the absence of social differentiation. The consequence of the absence of social differentiation—of this survival strategy—was that primitive thought was obsessed with social structure, that is, kinship, and that kinship structures were the only means they had available to order the world that surrounded them: nature thus was organized according to kinship principles (Durkheim 1912).

29. The best book on Levy-Bruhl is Keck (2008).

There is little literature on the discovery of society as a French event. However, see Peter Wagner's splendid essay on the rejection of the term "society" by German Staatswissenschaften "An Entirely New Object of Consciousness, of Volition, of Thought" (1999).

30. One could also list here the sole American anthropologist of the first half of the twentieth century who actively participated in this debate, Paul Radin. His book *The Method and Theory of Ethnology* was a powerful critique of Lévy-Bruhl—and his *Primitive Man as Philosopher* was his response. Interestingly, Radin asked John Dewey to write a preface: in a way, Dewey's pragmatism was to Radin what Wittgenstein's ordinary language philosophy was to British social anthropology. From Frédéric Keck I learned that Dewey in turn learned from Lévy-Bruhl. Apparently, Dewey's *How We Think* was partly echoing Lévy-Bruhl's *How Natives Think*.

After World War II, Clifford Geertz's cultural anthropology, relying on Susan Langer's rendering of Cassirer's *Philosophy of Symbolic Form* (heavily indebted to Lévy-Bruhl) could be understood as a contribution to the discussion on "primitive thought." However, neither Geertz nor, later, Marshall Sahlins was concerned with thought or the categories of mind. Instead Geertz was concerned with "scripts" and Sahlins with "cultural categories."

31. A set of qualifying remarks:

(1) Of course, one could list others. But "completeness" is not my aim: I merely mean to make visible a pattern and to provide a list of the most prominent names.

(2) What about Michel Foucault? I think Foucault defies the pattern: he is not a philosopher of the human but an empirically inclined, historically oriented researcher.

(3) I leave aside here the crossover area between philosophy and psychology.

(4) If one's ambition were to be exhaustive, one would also have to mention the significance of Wittgenstein's ordinary language philosophy for Evans-Pritchard's implicitly critical reply to Rivers's suggestion that the primitive cannot think in the abstract.

(5) And one would have to mention Paul Radin's still extraordinary *Primitive Man as Philosopher* (1927). While the significance of Wittgenstein for British social anthropology has frequently been alluded to, the relevance of Dewey for American anthropology has hardly been recognized. See footnote 25 above.

32. For example, the study of primitive thought is primarily a reflection of the philosophy of modernity, a philosophy that divided the whole of humanity into the nonmoderns (primitives, potentially incapable of rational thought) and the moderns (grounded in rational thought). And the effort to render visible the universal existential and moral grounds of what it means to be human has been contingent on the emergence of a general, time and place independent concept (abstraction) called "the human," that emerged in Europe between the 1630s and the 1830s (see chapter 2).

33. Arthur Kleinman, Michael Jackson, and Veena Das, introduction to *The Ground Between* (2014), footnote 1.

34. The reference is to Fassin's essay "The Parallel Lives of Anthropology and Philosophy" (2014).

35. The reference here is to the emergence of medical anthropology (Kleinman), to research on social suffering (Kleinman, Lock, and Das), and to the recent call (Fassin) for a moral anthropology.

36. I am greatly indebted here to many conversations with Paul Rabinow (see in particular Rabinow 2003).

37. One could even say that this kind of philosophical anthropology has no more need for philosophy as such; it has begun to understand itself as an empirical philosophy of a sort; it is interested in the philosophical fragments that, as concepts, structure the nitty-gritty domains of life, philosophical fragments that never stand still, that mutate, sometimes faster, sometimes slower, that ceaselessly break open new grounds.

38. "Or, comme dit Pline, chacun est à soi même une très bonne discipline. Ce n'est pas ici ma doctrine, s'est mon étude." Yet, said Pliny, each one of us is a very good challenge for ourself. This is not my theory. This is my exercise. Michel de Montaigne. *Essais.*

And as exercise, anthropology produces an anti-crisis ethos—or calm (Roitman 2013).

39. See my "As if Theory is the only Form of Thinking and Social Theory the only Form of Critique" (Rees 2011) and as well the forthcoming edited volume *Anthropology BSST (Beyond Society and Social Theory)* that I am currently working on. I also refer to Strathern 1988.

40. I think of the always-new subtitle that George Marcus and James Clifford gave to *Writing Culture.*

41. If I hold on to this term that is partly because this practice of *thinking about thought* is reminiscent of a millennia-old practice described by authors such as Paul Rabbow and Pierre Hadot—and so brilliantly rendered contemporary by such authors as Michel Foucault or Katja Vogt.

42. It is just this incapacity for abstracting thinking, Rivers added (1900:82), that made him devise the genealogical method: "The great value of the genealogical method is that it enables one to study abstract problems, on which the savage's ideas are vague, by means of concrete facts, of which he is a master."

43. See (Rivers 1900, 1910; Lévy-Bruhl 1910, 1922, 1926, 1952; Evans-Pritchard 1929, 1933, 1937, 1940; Durkheim and Mauss 1902; Durkheim 1912; Mauss 1931, [1938] 1950; Lévi-Strauss 1962; Bachelard 1934, 1938, [1949] 1966, 1953; Canguilhem 1994, 2000, 2005; Foucault 1966, 1969).

44. Of things? Yes, of things: for what, ultimately, is the real if not some undifferenti-ated mass, some say? So that whatever we identify as thing is actually constituted by the system of thought by which we, without knowing it, live.

Some even go as far as suggesting that the system determines what, at a given time, is possible.

45. And no one has helped me more to understand this than Fritz W. Kramer.

46. I think of Piet Mondrian's abstract—but entirely concrete—renderings of Cézanne.

One could, perhaps, as well refer to Tim Ingold (2017).

47. Another, complimentary line of thinking about thinking has been recently ren-dered visible brilliantly by Stefan Helmreich in "Election's Reverb: An Interview with Stefan Helmreich" accessible at https://culanth.org/fieldsights/1011-election-s-reverb-an-interview-with-stefan-helmreich. Helmreich points to Donna Haraway's phrase "think we must" (2016, 12), and to Marilyn Strathern (1992), Benjamin Wurgaft (2015), and Virginia Woolf (1938).

48. Fieldwork often requires follow-up research: years of reading, spent in libraries or archives, of nitty-gritty reconstruction.

"OF" THE HUMAN (AFTER "THE HUMAN")

1. According to Anna Tsing, "'Man' does not mean humans, but a particular kind of being invented by Enlightenment thought and brought into operation by modernization and state regulation and other related things"; quoted in Haraway et al. 2016, 7.

2. Even if most anthropologists allow for change—the emergence of new forms of bodily experiences, of new forms of politics, of subjectivity, and so on—their conception of change is such that it ultimately holds on to the universals that make their analyses meaningful: the body, politics, subjectivity, and so on.

3. As Michel Foucault asked in one of his lectures (Foucault 2008b:3), "How to allow for an analysis that doesn't ground in universals?"

4. The term "organism" first appears in Stahl (1695). For an excellent overview on how it further developed, see Cheung (2008).

5. W. W. Keen quoted in Schlich (2016). It may sound counterintuitive, but most languages that have been recorded by anthropologists seem to not have had a classical concept of the body, understood as an anatomical or physiological universal that marks the basis of all human existence. They may have words for the torso, legs, arms, or skin; indeed, often they have several words for "skin," as in "skin that protects" or the "skin that is injured." But they don't have an abstract concept of the body as such, that is, of the abstract and universal body independent of an individual, as it emerged in Europe in the eighteenth and nineteenth centuries. The best introduction is still Bruno Snell's *The Discovery of the Mind*, published originally in German as *Die Entdeckung des Geistes* (1946).

6. An anthropology "of" the human/after "the human" opens up the past—by liberat-ing it from historical studies that are organized by recent concepts unwittingly treated as universal—as well as the present (and the future).

7. This is, according to Diderot, the purpose of an encyclopedia: "Le but d'une encyclopédie est de rassembler les connaissances éparses sur la surface de la terre, d'en exposer le système général aux hommes avec qui nous vivons, et de le transmettre aux hommes qui viendront après nous" (Diderot 1755).

8. I quote Diderot according to the online version of the original edition of the Encyclopédie (last assessed on February 1, 2018), http://encyclopédie.eu/index.php /science/1111734492-philosophie/1219172107-encyclopedie.

9. Diderot, Encyclopédie, http://encyclopédie.eu/index.php/science/1111734492 -philosophie/1219172107-encyclopedie.

10. The literature on the concept of "the human" and the concepts in place to stabilize it is sparse. A beginning was arguably made by Foucault's *The Order of Things* ([1966] 1990). The German philosopher Odo Marquard published a short essay on the emergence of the concept "anthropology" in the history of European thought (Marquardt 1973). Heidegger's "The Age of the World Picture" ([1938] 1977) was arguably a critical reference for both of them. Bits and pieces for a history of the human can be found in Koselleck (1979, 2000, 2002, 2006, 2010).

11. It is hardly an exaggeration to say that the distinction between nature and "the human" as Diderot explicitly formulated it was the most significant tool for the invention of "the human" in mid-eighteenth-century France. Take, for example, Rousseau's *Discours sur l'inégalité* (Rousseau 1755). In this book, written in 1754 and published in 1755, Rousseau not only offers a critique of civilization in the name of nature, but by suggesting that the emergence of human civilization can be traced to the very moment when humans ceased being part of the natural world, he also constructs one of the first universal histories of "the human." Or take Voltaire's *Essai sur les moeurs et les esprit des nations*, which was first published in 1756 (Voltaire [1756] 1829). One of the key organizing principles of Voltaire's history of the French nation from the days of Charlemagne to his time was the distinction between nature and civilization. And, if the suggestion that history begins at just the moment when humans leave the natural cosmos behind was still implicit in his *Essai*, then the opposition between the natural world and the human world had become one of the key arguments of his *La philosophie de l'histoire* (Voltaire 1765). This latter work expanded beyond Europe and the French and told the history of humanity, from the savages to the barbarians to the civilized. Or consider Tourgout, Condillac, Maupertuis, Malherbe, Condorcet—the list of those who contributed to the invention of "the human" is long.

12. I quote according to the online edition of Kant's second critique (last assessed on February 1, 2018): http://gutenberg.spiegel.de/buch/kritik-der-reinen-vernunft-2 -auflage-3502/3.

13. Note that Kant's was a philosophical—or epistemological—and not a neuronal argument.

14. Kant also makes plain that what he calls a priori has nothing to do with experience, as if the forms of knowledge would get more refined over time. On the contrary, Kant insists that any experience is already contingent on these a priori conditions, which he considers as universal, as time-and-place independent.

15. The one place where Kant says that the question in which all of philosophy culmi-

nates is "Was ist der Mensch?" is his lectures on logic, which are available only through student excerpts. The three questions that precede the culminating one—What can I know? What can I do? What can I hope for?—already appear in the *Kritik der reinen Vernunft*. On Kant's philosophy as principally concerned with the human, see especially Brandt 2014, who points out that the question Was ist der Mensch? actually is at odds with Kant's argument and may well have been added by the student who compiled the excerpt. By the late eighteenth century, thus, the whole world had become contingent on the human. Kant's oeuvre marked the 'completion' of the anthropocentric epistemology, which has been constitutive of modernity—and as well of the human sciences.

I add that what I describe here was hardly a detached philosophical discourse. The work of Diderot and d'Almbert must be understood in the context of the struggles to question absolutism, which they—and many others—understood as the challenge to invent a new form of politics, one not focused on kings and their glory but on what was to them a new and exciting category: the human. This was, literally, revolutionary work. In a way, the whole *Encyclopédie* was—just as the invention of the philosophy of history, which happened in parallel—one massive effort to construct an anthropocentric conception of the world and to celebrate it as a breakthrough, and as a liberation (which no doubt it was). The aim was to explain that "the human"—whether in China or India, whether in France or Germany—was constitutive of the political and philosophical realities in which they lived, with the implication that if they created it, they could change it.

In Germany this took a somewhat different form. Kant's work on anthropology is impossible to understand without the rise of the bourgeoisie.

It is through a conceptual analysis of these events that one can appreciate the emergence of a novel epistemic formation in Europe in the final decades of the eighteenth century: the emergence of a general conceptualization of "the human" that allowed one to explain many different life forms as variations of a human theme; that would allow one to make visible a continuum of experiences across time and space.

16. But hasn't Kant's philosophy been repeatedly critiqued by critical thinkers over the last 250 years? It has, so often indeed that it is impossible to provide a list of the many critical rejections here. But it seems fair to say that the vast majority of the critiques of Kant have concerned his transcendental philosophy rather than his conception of philosophy as anthropology. This is to say that what has been exposed to critique is Kant's suggestion that the conditions of knowledge as he described them transcend time and space and are universal. Consequently, his transcendental a priori has been replaced by a historical a priori (most famously perhaps by Michel Foucault), by a cultural a priori (the last in a long line of vehement cultural anthropologists who have forcefully insisted on culture a priori was probably Marshall Sahlins), or by a social a priori (Durkheim had famously described his work as a sociologization of Kant—and it seems fair to argue that neither Pierre Bourdieu nor his successors, say Boltanski or Thévenot, have exceeded this project). If anything, then, these critical replacements have been an affirmation of the human rather than a critique of it.

17. How have humans thought about and lived in the world before the birth of "the human"? At least in seventeenth-century Europe the focus was on a natural, cosmological order. The assumption was that there is a natural order of the world that precedes the

human, an order not established by humans. On the contrary, humans had their place within this order. In the middle of the eighteenth century, with the emergence of the argument—probably nurtured by the dramatic increase of travel reports about foreign, faraway life forms—that humans, even if they didn't know about it, were themselves the authors of the order they lived in, the idea of a natural, timeless cosmos began to crumble. A good way to picture what happened is to think about the emergence of the central perspective in painting, which marks a human-centric way of organizing the world.

18. For a different critique of the concept of the human and of culture, see the work of Sylvia Wynter: a great overview of her work is offered by Wynter (2000) and Wynter (2014). I have gained significantly from Wynter's writings—and yet depart from her solution. In my reading, Wynter severs the culture concept from the Western, male, bourgeois definitions of culture and then rethinks it from the perspective of the (African) diaspora. That is, Wynter, in principle, holds on to the idea that humans are cultural beings—while I emphasize the historicity of the configuration of the human as cultural being.

19. I am hardly the first to ask this question. For example, two authors that immediately come to mind are Louis Althusser and Michel Foucault (whose work I discuss in the below digression on "Anti-Humanism"). However, already decades before Althusser and Foucault, in early twentieth-century European art, there was a powerful movement to abandon the human. Apollinaire wrote (1980 [1913]), "Avant tout, les artistes sont des hommes qui veulent devenir inhumains. Ils cherchent péniblement les traces de l'inhumanité." José Ortega y Gasset ([1925] 1962) wrote about "*la deshumanización del arte*." And Theodore Adorno wrote in his posthumous *Ästhetische Theorie* (1970), "Treue hält Kunst den Menschen allein durch Inhumanität gegen sie." Some may want to see Nietzsche quoted here, however, Wolfgang Welsch, in particular, has shown that Nietzsche's Übermensch is an anthropological conception.

I am not referring here to writings of the posthumanists. I find I could write with Donna Haraway (2008, 16–17) the idea of an anthropology "of" the human / after "the human" "to be a much richer web than any of the posthumanisms on display after (or in reference to) the ever-deferred demise of man. I never wanted to be a posthuman, or a posthumanist, any more than I wanted to be a postfeminist. For one thing, urgent work still remains to be done in reference to those who must inhabit the troubled categories of woman and human, properly pluralized, reformulated, and brought into constitutive intersection with other asymmetrical differences." What is at stake, Haraway adds, quoting Karen Barad, is "not getting beyond one troubled category for a worse one even more likely to go postal" (Haraway 2008, 16–17).

20. The irreducible openness provoked by the break with "the human"—when the real is released from the already thought and known—would be immediately exhausted by a new set of normative (foundational) claims.

An anthropology that evolves around instances in which events in the present overflow (the term is borrowed from Michel Callon) the conceptual presuppositions that have hitherto structured the present—or constituted its reality—cannot afford such a replacement approach. It cannot afford it as it would negate the very possibility of the openness it is interested in: the irreducible openness that can be found when an event cuts loose the real from the form of thought that until recently contained it, the nonteleological movement that rules in the openness in which no new conceptual structure has yet emerged that could give directionality to this movement, could exhaust it.

For an anthropology interested in instances of escape, it would be a fatal mistake to replace one normative framework with another one.

21. One can care about humanity by decentering it.

22. Take, for example, an anthropological study of the release of tiny CO_2 bubbles that have been frozen in ice for thousands of years (perhaps, in form of a fieldwork with ice scientists in the arctic). What if the task of (one kind of) anthropology would consist in rendering visible the comprehension—the beauty—of the world that emerges from the study of these CO_2 bubbles (rather than in pointing out that the scientific knowledge of these bubbles is socially grounded, which ultimately amounts to a reduction of the world to the human)? A world so vast and so old that "the human" shrinks and shrivels, that the epistemic anthropocentrism transported by "the human" becomes as ridiculous as ludicrous, that humans are displaced from the center and become little more than a late comer to the history of the Earth, an add on (if a destructive one). Could one make the statement that the constitution of the real that ice—melting ice—allows for escapes the anthropological certainties (the definitions of the human) that have silently structured anthropology? With the consequence that ice—melting ice—brings into view that (and how) the present outgrows—escapes—the (decoding) vocabulary anthropologists have (had) at their disposal? And could one argue that precisely this 'escape' undermines and tears open anthropology—and thereby allows one/compels one to learn to think differently?

The challenge would be to use the study of melting ice to expose "the human," to ask what new, what other ways of thinking the human—of living a life—are emerging from the study of ice. To be more precise, the challenge would be to make the mismatch between reality as constituted by ice and reality as constituted by the human a (if not the only) central focus of one's analysis. (This, while at the same time striving to avoid making the mistake of then presenting this new/other anthropology—one that grounds in melting ice rather than in "the human—as the new normative.)

23. Such an anthropology of bacteria has no need to provide bacteria with agency or intentionality. There is no necessity to extend the concepts that were constitutive of human exceptionalism to the nonhuman world (what an odd universalization of the human it would be to make bacteria—or archaea or eukaryotes—humans among humans). Bacteria are literally world making, for all living things. Anthropology can bring this world making into view and can ask questions of it that bacteriologists don't ask: questions about being in the world, about relationality, about the normal and the pathological, about things human.

24. As Peter Crane writes in his extraordinary *Gingko* (2013, 4–5), "For almost all of its long tenure on our planet gingko inhabited a world without people, and for much of that time, a world very different from that of today. For tens of millions of years it lived alongside plants and animals that are long since extinct. Several kinds of gingkolike trees watched as our ancestors transformed from reptiles to mammals. Fossil gingko leaves are known from every continent. The prehistory of gingko goes back to before the Atlantic Ocean existed and before the southern continents broke from Antarctica and went their own ways."

25. See Stefan Helmreich's project on waves, "The Water Next Time: Changing Wave-scapes in the Anthropocene" (Helmreich 2014).

On matsutake, see Anna Tsing (2015).

On methane bubbles in the Greenland ice sheet, see the forthcoming dissertation research of Julianne Yip.

On Ebola, see Vinh-Kim Nguyen's recent work, for example, Nguyen (2014).

On snails, see my own research project "The Snail and the Human," a first sketch of which I have provided in Rees (2014b).

On Hurricane Katrina, see Vincanne Adams (2013).

On the neoliberal social, see Stephen Collier (2011) and James Ferguson (2015).

One more example: take the set of genes—the COP9 complex—that humans and plants share and that open up an unexpected middle ground between plants and humans. Wouldn't it be intriguing to explore this middle ground, to learn to think about things human from its perspective?

On L1 jumping genes see Rees (2016).

On SpaceX, see Lisa Messeri (2016) and on Mars see Vertesi (2015).

26. "And critique?" I hear someone say. "What becomes of critique if one gives up the social? Even the political? How to critically engage without any stable positions?"

To drop "the human" is hardly the end of critical inquiry. On the contrary, it is itself an act of critique. It is true, the exposure of established concepts and categories renders easy gestures to established scripts difficult; it requires learning to think anew. It requires the reinvention, for each project, of what critique could mean and why it matters.

27. I think, for example, of the work of Stephen Collier (2011) and James Ferguson (2010, 2015). Collier and Ferguson both noted, independently from one another, that the genuine forms of social welfare the neoliberal reforms they studied produced—the former in post-Soviet Russia, the latter in post-Apartheid South Africa—were such that they defied the concept of the social on which the social sciences and along with them social critique and social theory were built. Struck by their discovery they both began (1) to write the history of the social as we knew it—thereby exposing its historicity and depriving it of its givenness—and (2) to elaborate the possibility of a study "of" the social/after "the social." In terms of an analysis of movement / in terms of movement: they used their recognition of the inadequacy of the social of the social sciences—the inadequacy of the depiction of the form human living together takes—to give contours to the new/different concept of the social that emerged at the time of their fieldwork.

28. It seems to me that this is where I may differ from Tim Ingold's (2014, 2017) "ontological commitment" to the world: "behind" the cool abstraction of "normal science" he discovers the really real—thereby granting his account the privilege of being ontologically true. Though where does the certainty of truth come from?

As soon as Ingold begins to articulate the really real he almost inevitably—or so it seems to me—reduces it to a scheme that is contingent, could be otherwise, is not more privileged than the schemes he critiques.

To avoid misunderstandings: I share the commitment to curiosity and care: but the form my curiosity and care take is hesitation, is doubt, is skepticism in the ancient sense: an attention to that which gets lost, which cannot be subsumed. My work is an effort to render visible (Guattari and Deleuze) the "always new": is the effort to ceaselessly reconstitute uncertainty (as the highest good).

29. Indeed, there is no doubt a correspondence between the idea of an anthropology "of" the human on the one hand, and Hacking's "Making up People" (1986) and Rabinow's "Midst Anthropology's Problems" (2002) on the other. It is as if they pushed in a direction very similar to the one I am pushing—and, of course, years before me (Hacking's paper was written in 1983, Rabinow's in 2001). And yet, it seems to me as if there is a perhaps subtle but far-reaching difference.

30. Rabinow's Deleuzian epilogue to *French DNA* (1999) is perhaps an exception: On the one hand, the emphasis on assemblages is a shift away from the intentional subject and allows one to understand the emergence of new logoi as the unforeseeable result of a series of events that point in different directions. On the other hand, it remains concerned with human reality alone.

31. On the tape I continue to explain this: "I would like to add that this is exactly where I differ from, for example, Bruno Latour and his followers: He/they have replaced one grid, one scaffold, with another one which he/they claim is more true, which is closer to the really real. Here the human, there actor-networks understood as nature-cultures. Even if it sounds a bit harsh, to me this replacement attitude is self-deception. It is the construction of a new universalism, which transports all the problems the old universalism they critiqued transported as well. What interests me instead, I mean in my research, are the very concrete derailments that emerge from chance recognitions, accidental findings, unexpected observations, etc. In that sense I have no program. Or so I like to think." Again laughter follows.

32. "My aim," Michel Foucault wrote in 1969, "is to define a method of historical analysis freed from the anthropological theme" (Foucault [1969] 1972, 17). And Louis Althusser, four years earlier, in 1965, had already put forth the view of "humanism as an ideology."

On antihumanism, see Geroulanos (2010).

33. In the text he shows that the young Marx was a humanist, that his aim was to fight the alienation of the human from human nature: Marx hoped to return the human to its human nature. However, around 1845 Marx made what was, according to Althusser, a most significant "discovery": that the concept of the human he had grounded his politics in was a generalization—he writes "essentialization"—of the bourgeois subject.

34. Althusser adds that bourgeois philosophy as it emerged in the late eighteenth century "depended in all of its domains and arguments on a problematic of human nature" ([1965] 2005, 227).

35. "Marx's materialism excludes the empiricism of the subject" (Althusser [1965] 2005, 228). "Marx established a new problematic, a new systematic way of asking questions of the world, new principles and a new method" (Althusser [1965] 2005, 229).

36. A theory of history that would be free from "the sovereignty of the subject, and the twin figures of anthropology and humanism." (Foucault [1969], 1972, 12, 16).

37. The quotes are all taken from the "Introduction" of *The Archeology of Knowledge*.

38. His big archaeological discovery, presented in *The Order of Things*, was that "the human" is precisely the product of one such radical epistemic shift, which occurred

around 1800. And his hope was that the epistemic formation that gave rise to the human would soon dissolve and disappear.

39. On general history see especially Foucault (1971, 9–10).

40. This is hardly a critique of Althusser and Foucault: What I offer here, rather, is a differentiation. Althusser meant to get away from bourgeois ideology and to ground Marxist philosophy of history in materialism; and Foucault tried to escape the generalization of the subject and to come up with "a new general theory" for analyzing history epistemologically. Neither one of them was concerned with what I have called the open.

41. See also Rees (2010a).

42. And with Tim Ingold (2016) one could say that theories produce worlds: worlds of abstraction and generalities that render the world uninhabitable.

43. No doubt, the emergence of an anthropology not concerned with humans has been critical for me, has allowed me to give sharper contours to the idea of an anthropology after "the human." That being said, there are aspects of multispecies explorations that are, if looked at from the perspective of an anthropology after "the human" as I have thought to develop it, somewhat unfortunate. Indeed, it occasionally seems as if some multispecies anthropologies unwittingly hold on to "the human," for example, when concepts like *agency* or *subjectivity* or *intentionality* or *the social* are used, as if nothing were more evident, to describe animal life.

It is not, I think, that I don't understand the reason for this expansion. But my curiosity points in another direction: I am interested in the history of these concepts—and in how the recognition of a resemblance between humans and nonhumans undermines them and thereby opens up a new, different space for which we still lack terms and concepts. I wonder how the bringing face-to-face of, say, snails and humans opens up an epistemic space that cannot be assessed by these human universals, how it derails them and thereby opens up new, yet to be explored venues for thinking or for living. Differently put, I am interested in what this encounter does to the human—and also to the snail (Rees 2014b).

One version of the reproduction of "the human" is the somewhat uncritical expansion of critical social theory to the nonhuman world. Perhaps the most prominent venue in which categories invented to describe the (supposedly) uniquely human are uncritically extended to the nonhuman world is behavioral research on animals, specifically, animal intelligence. Whatever concept philosophers invented to define the distinctively human, from thought and empathy to subjectivity or politics, from existential questions to self-awareness and a sense of humor and the decoupling of sex from reproduction (and much more): in their (understandable) effort to prove human exceptionalism wrong, behavioral researchers often enroll animals in human categories rather than question these categories as such, in their validity for humans.

44. I think in particular of Haraway's *Primate Visions* (1990) and Latour's *We Have Never Been Modern* ([1991]1993), two thorough problematizations of the nature/culture divide in terms of hybrid nature-cultures made up of humans and nonhumans. However, I think as well of Haraway's "A Cyborg Manifesto" ([1984] 1991), which declared that "the boundary between human and animals is thoroughly breached" (151), and of Latour's *The Pasteurization of France* (1988), with its exceptional witty critique of the category of society in the name of microbes. It was above all the work of Haraway and

Latour that has made it possible to radically rethink what the human sciences are or could be about.

45. For example, Tsing (2015) is an exploration of the possibility of an anthropology that thrives on indeterminacy (20, 23, 37–38, 46–47, and passim) rather than on knowledge (that forgets the provinciality of its own condition of possibility). What is more, the book is an exploration of a new concept of knowledge, one that doesn't ground in "summing up" or "scaling up," but that still provides insights (33–34, 37–38).

I read Stefan Helmreich's conception of "athwart" (2015, 90–105) as an exciting attempt to allow for the possibility of nonfoundational research—of research that neither is grounded in nor attempts to build foundations.

I would also like to point out here how meticulously Kath Weston in her *Animate Planet: Making Visceral Sense of Living in a High-Tech Ecologically Damaged World* (2017) avoids ontological claims or conclusions: when she elaborates on animacies and intimacies, she explores contemporary ways of living—and not ontology-based corrections of an error called modernity.

A second difference between ontologists and multi-species anthropologists one could mention is that most of the ontologists work in classical modern ethnographic settings, while many multispecies authors are, from a classical ethnographic perspective, working in modern settings.

46. Let's mention at least in passing that Mol's critique of epistemology is somewhat odd, at least when it comes to the historical epistemology that emerges from the writings of Bachelard, Canguilhem, Rheinberger, and others. These authors are neither out there as judges of the accuracy of knowledge nor to provide a general foundation of knowledge that would be accurate to nature. On the contrary, they are adamant that whatever is known is contingent on the technical and methodological circumstances of its being known. But in sharp contrast to Mol, these authors haven't done away with the idea of a world that exists independent of humans, a world that humans can successively get to know. In other words, for these authors a conceptual analysis is not in opposition—in a competition with—scientific knowledge production.

47. Mol cites as well Michel Callon and, especially, John Law.

48. How Latour can then allow microbes to participate in this network is a whole other question, which he addresses poorly, and at which point his ANT alternative collapses.

49. Let me add that this critique of Mol's humorless reading of Latour doesn't take anything away from what has arguably been a most important contribution of her book: the expansion of the scope of the concept of practice, especially in STS. Before Mol, the concept of practice was largely defined by laboratory studies and narrowly focused on experimentation. With Mol's work on performance, the concept of practice was cut loose from the important but somewhat narrow focus on experimentation. Mol's contribution was paralleled by the work of Charis Thompson (2007).

50. Indeed, in his *Politics of Nature*, Latour ([1999] 2004) explicitly celebrated Descola for arguing that a precondition of a comparative anthropology is to recognize the nature concept as a Western peculiarity that needs to be dropped if one wants to bring into view non-Western societies that don't have a concept for nature and whose societies include humans as well as nonhumans.

51. For more than a decade I have worked on the discovery that thousands of new neurons are born every day in the adult human brain. This discovery was first made in 1998. If one takes Mol's argument seriously, then it amounts to the odd suggestion that no neurons were born in human brains before 1998.

52. To critique Mol or Latour doesn't imply upholding a naïve positivism, according to which arteriosclerosis (or bacteria) objectively exist as discrete conditions or entities. Arguably, what bacteria are, for humans, depends on the concepts and practices in place to know them. The critical remark here merely concerns Mol's straightforward suggestion that arteriosclerosis—or Latour's ironic suggestion that bacteria—are simply the product of human knowledge practices. That seems a gross over estimation of the significance of human ways of knowing + doing.

53. Durkheim and Mauss, in their *Primitive Classification* (1963), don't offer such an argument. On the contrary, they maintain a strict anthropocentric epistemology, that is, they operate with a strict dualism that distinguishes between the human here and the natural world there. "The primitives" merely *use* their kinship terminology to structure the natural world.

54. Of particular pertinence here is what one could call Tom Boellstorff's (2016) "provincialization" of the ontological turn. Boellstorff, a careful reader of classic modern ethnographies, notes that the notion of anthropology upheld by the authors of the ontological term is specific to a Cambridge/UK-based understanding of "social anthropology as a comparative project." As he beautifully—disarmingly—remarks, Franz Boas, for example, harbored a general "doubt of the possibility of establishing valid categories for the comparison of cultural phenomena."

Boellstorff silently (and brilliantly) repeats—and reinforces—an earlier American critique of British social anthropology. Here I am particularly referring to Clifford Geertz (in his turn toward culture and cultural history, which he explicitly understood as a critique of British social anthropology; see Handler's 1991 interview with Geertz and David Schneider—first with his culturalization of kinship in 1968 and then with his full-blown critique of the very idea of kinship in 1984).

55. It is interesting here to think through Kohn's very thoughtful work from the perspective of Kath Weston's (2017) differentiation of "animism" (a highly problematic term that served to mark supposed primitivism and political asymmetry) and "animacy" (a self-conscious living in close intimacy with animals, plants, and ecosystems). Is it fair to argue that Kohn's work, by virtue of expanding human concepts to the nonhuman world, is ultimately a form of animism, not of animacy.

56. A similar critique has been formulated with much more political vehemence by Bessire and Bond (2014a, 2014b). I quote at length: "In reference to those critical predecessors who are often erased from the intellectual genealogies of self-proclaimed ontologists—such as Frantz Fanon, Hannah Arendt, Raymond Williams, Judith Butler, and Michel Foucault—we suggest that the figure of the ontological may itself operate as a mode for reifying the very effects it claims to overturn. Indeed, it seems as if much of the ontological turn is premised on skipping over an entire generation of anthropologists that took up these same problems and worked them out in very different ways, whether in the cultural refractions of capitalist world systems (Mintz 1985, Wolf 1982), in the

labored dimensions of colonial categories (Comaroff 1985, Stoler 1989), or in feminist and queer critiques of structuralist binaries (Martin 1987, Ortner 1974)."

One could easily come up with a whole library's worth of further names, from Angela Davis and Sylvia Wynter to Lila Abu-Lughod, Tim Mitchell, Donna Haraway, Fritz Kramer, Johannes Fabian, Arjun Appadurai, and many more.

Bessire and Bond suggest here the erasure, by ontologists, of half a century of political critique of the figure of the primitive. Why this erasure? Because to do away with the figure of the primitive—and with "feminists and halfies," to quote Abu-Lughod's article "Writing against Culture" (1991)—would undermine the very condition of the possibility of the ontological turn. In the words of Bessire and Bond (2014a, 442), "The analytic allegiances wrapped up in the ontological turn seem uniquely unable to examine the fraught conditions of their own flourishing." That is, of the reliance on the premodern as the original, as the place were wisdom was preserved. "The pertinent questions of how difference comes to matter and what kinds of difference are allowed to matter are pointedly left unaddressed. What we insist on is that the worlds conjured by such a project do not seem new at all. Rather, they appear frighteningly familiar."

In his article "For Whom the Ontology Turns" (2016), Tom Boellstorff offers a similar critique of the ontological turn and its unacknowledged primitivism. Boellstorff's suggestion to the ontologists is that they begin with the critical step of "de-ontologizing the concept of difference" they are operating with. Of course, if the ontologists were to give up on radical ontological alterity (silently mediated by society), there would be no point (for the ontologists) in talking about ontology anymore.

57. This is not meant as wholesale critique. There are most excellent works that reflect on—or subversively play with—these inversions/relations; see, for example, (Povinelli 2016, Tsing 2015, Helmreich 2009, Raffles 2011).

58. Why "existence at all"? The problem with any ontology is that, even if it seeks to allow for an otherwise, it must reduce the world to a scheme. Wouldn't one need, instead, to expose ontology? And to thereby simultaneously open up the many worlds that existed before ontology and after ontology (independent of being)?

59. This passage could not have been written without Alessandra Ponte's work; see especially Ponte (2014, 169–221).

60. Marilyn Strathern (1972, 1988, 1991, 1992a) has brilliantly avoided just this pitfall of ontologization: In sharp contrast to many of her followers, she has consistently refused to articulate a theory of the relation as the true ontological ground of being in the world. On the contrary, she has consistently de-ontologized the relation (e.g., 1995) and has rendered (and used) it as a functional, descriptive tool that can be used as experimental technique that generates unexpected surprises (e.g., 1992b).

61. From here, it is perhaps but a small step to Michel Foucault's *Les mots et les choses*— words *and* things, itself an attempt to think about the historicity of "the middle" in non-anthropocentric terms—or to Marilyn Strathern's (in my reading radically) anti-ontological studies of the "in between" (1972) and "the relation" (1995). Why radically antiontological? Because Strathern seems to be at pains to never let her work on relations become anything more than a somewhat antisubstantive (and in that sense functional) tool for inquiry that she found.

1. I am also curious—but leave this for another time—if one couldn't, once anthropology is decoupled from ethnos, dissociate anthropological research from fieldwork? Is there any obvious reason why fieldwork would be the only, the sole, the authoritative form of anthropological knowledge production? I ask this as fieldwork enthusiast.

2. G. P. H. Normann (1785, 4n7). H. Fischer (1970, 176); and Stagl (1995, 237).

3. "Anthropological research" is a somewhat awkward category—one that is the outcome rather than the starting point of the history I am trying to write.

4. "Expedition" seems to have been derived from the "expedite" efforts to provide goods from elsewhere by ship.

5. See (Keay 1991; Gardner 1971; Lawson 2014; Philips 1961).

6. See (Cook 1967, Thomas 1996).

7. George Stocking, Jr.'s *Victorian Anthropology* (1987, 78–109) gives a most excellent overview of the varieties of travelers that were characteristic of nineteenth-century anthropology.

8. Stocking (1984, 1987, 1988).

9. Why didn't I mention, for example, the Spanish conquistadores? Or the French and English exploration of North America? My aim here was not to provide a list of every trip European travelers or explorers undertook. Instead, my aim has been to make visible a particular genre of scientific travel called "expedition." And the term—the genre— "expedition" seems to have developed largely with respect to the Pacific Ocean, and later with respect to inner Africa, South America, and the poles.

10. In 1895 Haddon had already published a study of the evolution of art, from first figurines to modern realism.

11. No one introduced the term "field" in any conceptual way. However, my broad reading adventures in the history of anthropology led me to think of the Torres Strait expedition as a kind of caesura: it was only with the publications of the reports from the Torres Strait expedition that the term "field" was used in a continuous fashion to describe the kind of science anthropology is or ought to be. Let me stress again, though, that this seemed to have happened in an implicit way, as the transfer of a term from one field to another.

12. Already in 1930 the Seligmans had published the first edition of *Races of Africa* (which was reissued several times until the mid-1960s).

13. "It is only, however, since leaving the islands, and while getting the data into order, that I have realized the many possibilities which I believe [the genealogical method] opens to the anthropologists" (Rivers 1900, 74).

14. For Rivers's efforts in genealogy, see volumes 5 and 6 of the Reports of the Cambridge Expedition to the Torres Strait. See as well his *The Todas* (1906) and his article "The Genealogical Method in Anthropological Inquiry" (1910).

15. I am grateful to Allan Young for our conversations about Rivers.

In his article in the *Journal of the Anthropological Institute of Great Britain and Ireland* (1900, 74), Rivers writes that he first began to recognize the "many possibilities [the genealogical] method opens to the anthropologists" in 1899, when, back in Cambridge, he began working through his notes. However, it was only his 1901–2 research among the Todas that allowed him to test the usefulness of the method.

The phrase "system of relations" is from Rivers (1910). On his "discovery," see Rivers (1906, 11–12; also chapter 20).

"System" and "organization" might well be the technical terms Rivers used most often in his 1906 book on the Todas.

16. The interest in social organization had been a topic in anthropology since at least the works of Lewis Henry Morgan (1871, 1877) and John McLennan (in 1865 and 1877), two lawyers who studied how societies—in the legal sense of the term—were organized in terms of legal rights and responsibilities. However, in my interpretation, Rivers powerfully departs from these older legal studies. Why? Because Rivers was not interested in a system of juridical rights and responsibilities—which leaves all nonlegal aspects of social life unmentioned—but in how kinship organized the whole of social life, including a sense of self.

17. See especially Rivers *Anthropology and Ethnology* (1922), which, on the one hand, is a rejection of evolutionary anthropology and, on the other, suggests that ethnology is a kind of history of cultural diffusion and social differentiation of the very early stages of human history.

18. Quote from Rivers (1912, 112).

The challenge of fieldwork was, as Rivers put it, "to get to the bottom of native custumes and modes of thought, and to record the results of inquiry in such a manner that they carry conviction." He added that this was possible only "by careful attention to method" (108).

19. Between 1906 and 1908, Radcliffe-Brown had repeatedly visited the Andaman Islands (located in the Indian Ocean). These visits were initially for his fellowship thesis at Trinity College at Cambridge and resulted in what one could describe as a classical nineteenth-century reconstruction of cultural history (he added a version of this cultural history as an appendix to his *Andaman Islanders*).

After his return to the United Kingdom, he was, until 1910, lecturing on anthropology in Cambridge and at the London School of Economics. According to William Edward Hanley Stanner (1956), it was during these years that Radcliffe-Brown discovered the writings of Durkheim and Mauss. If the writings of the French sociologists mattered to Radcliffe-Brown, they did so for two reasons. First, they resonated strongly with Rivers's systems approach but were more philosophically savvy. Second, they provided him with a way of theorizing questions that had concerned him since he first read Kropotkin's *Mutual Aid* ([1902] 1909), which lays out a theory of early social life as free of property (Stanner 1969).

This assemblage of questions (How is social cohesion in an anarchical state possible?) and conceptual tools (systems approach, social facts) led Radcliffe-Brown to return to the notes he had collected while on the Andamans to write *The Andaman Islanders*. See as well Kuper (2010).

An exceptionally good review of Radcliffe-Brown as teacher and thinker has been given by Walter Stanner (1956). See as well Eggan and Warner (1956).

For the relationship between Radcliffe-Brown and Rivers—Radcliffe-Brown had been Rivers's very first anthropology student—see Stocking 1984.

20. There are, of course, the special circumstances that led Malinowski to live among the Trobrianders: as citizen of Habsburg Austria he was considered a political enemy of the British Empire. The only way to escape encampment was to leave Australia and to live on the Trobriand Islands. As Malinowski had no financial means, however, he could not afford to live among the whites: he had to plant his tent among the natives. For the best background on the circumstances that led him to stay on Kiriwina, see M. Young 2004. For an excellent study of the effect of Malinowski's longer-than-usual stays among "the primitives," see Kramer (1977).

21. Malinowski is famous for having introduced the phrase "participant observation." However, given the focus of my essay, I stress that he was the first to use the term "fieldwork" in a systematic, technical manner.

22. Malinowski [1922] 2005. See Gellner's (1998) brilliant interpretation of Malinowski's work.

23. Malinowski [1922] 2005: 21, 60.

24. Of course, people traveled to faraway places, learned exotic languages, and wrote about foreign life forms long before Malinowski. And most certainly Malinowski (1922) was contingent on the Torres Straight expedition and even more so on the works of Seligman and especially Rivers (Kuklick 1991, 201; Stocking 1987, 1992; M. Young 2004). But I would stress that while Malinowski's formulation of fieldwork from 1922 was arguably contingent on the works of his predecessors, it is not reducible to it. I thus disagree with authors such as James Urry (1993), who doubt Malinowski's originality altogether. While I have profited from Urry's reading of Rivers, I see no reason to support Urry's iconoclasm: there is a perhaps subtle but still very far-reaching difference between Rivers's "the native also has a point" and Malinowski's "the native point of view." For example, compare Rivers's *History and Ethnology* (1922) with Malinowski's *Argonauts* (1922). The difference couldn't be starker: there is no necessary, no obvious way from Rivers's historical, diffusionist conception of ethnography to Malinowski's fieldwork-based ethnography.

25. Firth published *Primitive Economics* in 1929 and *We, the Tikopia* in 1936. Richards published *Hunger and Work in a Savage Tribe* in 1932. Powdermaker's *Life in Lesu* appeared in 1932. Schapera's *The Khoisan Peoples of South Africa* was published in 1930 and his *Handbook of Tswana Law* in 1938. Evans-Pritchard Azande book came out in 1937, and his *The Nuer* in 1940; Meyer Fortes, by training a psychologist, published *The Web of Clanship among the Tallensi* in 1945.

26. Fritz Kramer (1977) suggested that Malinowski's "synthetic ethnography" was reminiscent of Picasso's cubism.

27. It seems consequential, thus, that Radcliffe-Brown had little to contribute to the language of fieldwork Malinowski sought to provide. And indeed, in his early writings he used neither the term "field" nor the term "fieldwork." This is by no means meant as a critique of Radcliffe-Brown let alone as an effort to lower his enormous significance for anthropology in any way.

28. But what about American anthropology? Didn't Boas introduce fieldwork as method to American anthropology? He did not, as George Stocking, Jr., has made plain (1992, 14). Boas, like Malinowski, decoupled ethnography (in the old geographical sense) from evolutionary speculations. However, in sharp contrast to Malinowski, he seems to have maintained a geographical understanding of ethnography, one that was partially informed by German *Kulturgeschichte*. He certainly did not—nor, as far as I can tell, did his students—come up with the suggestion that the goal of ethnography is the collection of concrete episodes (Rivers, Malinowski) that would allow one to provide a glimpse of a single foreign society from the inside. Indeed, how far away from a Malinowski-style fieldwork/ethnography American anthropology was is nicely illustrated by a letter from Paul Radin to Edward Sapir (Radin 1998), in which he writes that the model that guides his research among the Winnebago is Jacob Burckhardt's *Kulturgeschichte der Renaissance in Italian*. I am afraid that the invention of fieldwork/ethnography was a British affair. American anthropology—just like French or German or Dutch or Scandinavian anthropology—largely continued (until after World War II) in an expedition-like style.

On American anthropology between 1888 and 1945, see the exceptionally helpful volumes edited by George Stocking, Jr. (1968, 2001).

29. Arguably, these studies could no longer be contained by an analytical vocabulary invented to get at the "underlying ideas" that organize faraway societies and their culture (as Malinowski put it in 1922, and as Geertz upheld in 1973 when he suggested that the life of the Balinese was organized by inarticulated scripts the ethnographer has to observe). The consequence was a *débordement*, an overflowing of the assumptions and presuppositions that had made fieldwork as ethnography a meaningful practice for almost a century.

30. The perhaps most powerful indicator of this interest in difference in time rather than in space has been the arrival of the concepts of the "emergent" and the "event" in anthropological inquiries. Exemplary here are Das 1996; M. Fischer 1999, 2004; Maurer 2005; and Rabinow 1996a, 1999.

31. My understanding of fieldwork is thoroughly informed by the work of George Marcus and Arjun Appadurai, who both, if in different ways, unbound fieldwork (I also refer to the works of James Ferguson and Akhil Gupta). However, I would maintain that while these works unbound fieldwork from space, they continued to frame fieldwork in spatial terms.

32. Another way of circumscribing the idea of a field science would be to describe it as a Wissenschaft that grounds in the primacy of the field (rather that in genealogies to which fieldwork is then a mere addendum or final chapter); that finds its questions, stories, and even theories in the field (and not in preset research questions or readings); that produces works that evolve essentially around the surprises and discoveries the field gives rise to.

33. An alternative way to capture the difference the anthropology after ethnos / interested in difference in time introduces into fieldwork is to say that it has mutated the concept of "surprise" that anthropologists work with. Again there is some important overlap: for both the spatially and the temporally oriented anthropologist, fieldwork

means the long-term immersion in the actual, everyday life of a particular group of actors with the explicit purpose of being surprised in one's thinking by what they do, by how they do it, and by how they think about what they do. This is to say that fieldwork is the (somewhat personalized) method for producing surprise—to generate insights one did not have and probably could not have had otherwise. However, in a most radical contrast, the fieldwork-based study of the new/different frames surprise not in spatial terms—as is the habit in much of sociocultural anthropology—but in temporal terms.

Put differently, the surprise generated by fieldwork into the new—into that which escapes the already thought and known—does not ground in the recognition that elsewhere it is different but rather in the insight that established concepts, ways of thinking, forms of knowing no longer work. Surprise consists in the experience that one's concepts don't work any longer—that an opening has occurred, a mutation, a rupture; that we live in a situation we have not yet learned to come to terms with (largely because the conceptual presuppositions implicit in the already existing concepts are inadequate to the new situation—and reform unlikely to do the job); a situation that unfolds beyond our established categories of thought, including (at least potentially) society and culture.

I tend to think—and realize that this is controversial—that a temporal concept/experience of surprise is potentially more powerful, insofar as it is more radical and all-encompassing than a spatial one. For example, the more traditional (spatial) challenge of ethnography has been to identify that which is different (the foreign) as a variant of the already known, that is, as variants of society and culture. In sharp contrast, the challenge of an anthropology interested in difference in time is to identify (or be identified by) that which cannot possibly be captured by the already known. The yet incommensurable, identified-through-surprise-generating derailments in the course of fieldwork—this is the core of fieldwork into the emergent. At stake is the difference today makes with respect to yesterday.

These surprises come in at least three forms. The first is thematic: one wishes to study neoliberalism in post-Soviet Russia or in contemporary South Africa—and is surprised that nothing conforms to what one has read (Collier 2011, Ferguson 2015); or one wishes to study Alzheimer's in India—and is derailed by the discovery that there is no Alzheimer's in South Asia (Cohen 2001). A second form of surprise is being led astray: say a fieldwork sets out to work on French biotechnology and ends up in a neuroscience lab—without ever having read anything about the brain—and then discovers that this lab is centrally involved in the formulation of a radically novel conception of the brain. A third kind of surprise is more discipline-specific: when one recognizes that well-established anthropological concepts, most notably "society" and "culture," are not adequate to capture the phenomenon in question.

34. George Marcus explained in a conversation with Tarek Elhaik on "Curatorial Designs in the Poetics and Politics of Ethnography Today" (2010): "In the mid 1990s I became interested in certain projects of installation and conceptual art that involved inquiry similar to fieldwork in their production. While I don't think ethnography is or should be the same as these art movement, my attraction to the latter captures something in terms of practice that I think ethnographic inquiry is lacking and very much needs."

It is interesting to note that, just at the time of the ethnographic turn in art, Marcus makes a distinction between fieldwork and ethnography—as if he wishes to 'rescue' anthropology from the ethnographic turn while simultaneously appreciating the possibility to converse with artists and to explore the unarticulated artistic potentialities of fieldwork as Wissenschaft.

The artist Fiamma Montezemolo (http://fiammamontezemolo.com) and the anthropologist Tarek Elhaik are at home in just this in between world—in between art as informed by fieldwork and fieldwork as an artistically informed anthropological Wissenschaft.

The consequence, beautifully, is that they both break with the significance of cultural difference and social identity and representation that plagued the ethnographic turn (which ultimately transported a primitivist conception of the other). Montezemolo explores the possibility of ethnography in the moment of its impossibility—and Elhaik curates the possibility of anthropology at just the time when this possibility ceases to exist. See as well Rabinow (2017).

35. Furthermore, it offers, if implicitly, a critique of the present in the name of a past that has probably never existed. As if all of classical modern ethnography grounded in the radical comprehension—in the practice—of anthropology as a radical field science that I outlined above! Can one really claim that when anthropologists studied descent lines, rituals, and myths, anthropology was practiced as the radical kind of field science that I outlined above? Or that the study of science and medicine has diluted the once intact idea of the primacy of the field? Theoretical inclinations, pre-articulated research questions, and historical narratives were certainly not absent in the supposedly good old days.

36. The first anthropologists to use "event" as a technical term to indicate temporal difference, to make it amenable to anthropological analysis, were Das (1996) and Rabinow (1996b). The earliest reference to "the emergent" is Michael Fischer (1999).

37. One could also mention "reconstruction," a term derived from Dewey (used by Collier 2011), and, of course, "genealogy" (which has been around since the late 1990s).

38. Obviously, I am hardly the first anthropologist to speak about assemblages. Paul Rabinow introduced the phrase "anthropology of assemblages" in 2003. Aihwa Ong and Stephen Collier, largely building on Rabinow, published an edited volume titled *Global Assemblages* in 2005.

In her 2015 *The Mushroom at the End of the World* Anna Tsing offered a version of an anthropology of assemblages that she explicitly juxtaposes to that of Rabinow on the one hand and that of Ong and Collier on the other.

39. Serres and Latour (1995).

On agencement, see Deleuze and Guattari (1987). A helpful comment on the agencement/assemblage relation/translation is provided by John Phillips (2006).

In a very interesting way the term "agencement" has been used by Michel Callon (2013, specifically 425–30).

40. Serres here also alludes to an earlier moment in their conversation, in which he explained his understanding of time thus: "If you take a handkerchief and spread it out in order to iron it, you can see in it certain fixed distances and proximities. If you sketch

a circle in one area, you can mark out nearby points and measure far-off distances. Then take the same handkerchief and crumple it, by putting it in your pocket. Two distant points suddenly are close, even superimposed. . . . Time . . . resembles this crumpled version much more than the flat, overly simplified one." Serres then goes on to say that we might "need the latter for measurements," but that if there is no point to "extrapolate from it a general theory of time. People usually confuse time and the measurement of time, which is a metrical reading on a straight line."

Serres's use of the term "contemporary" has led Paul Rabinow to design an "anthropology of the contemporary" (Rabinow 1999, 2003).

As I understand it, Rabinow's use of the terms assemblage and contemporary gained contour by his effort to refine Foucault's *history of the present* into an *anthropology of the recent past and the near future*, where the term contemporary replaces the term present/modernity and where the term assemblage replaces the term apparatus (for Rabinow, Foucault's dispositif has a longue durée, it is relatively stable, while assemblages are more tentative and short-lived: they might develop into a dispositive, but might as well dissolve just like that). On Rabinow's use of the term contemporary and as well on his use of the term assemblage see Rabinow (2003). See as well footnote 2 of chapter 4.

In contrast to Rabinow, to whom I am greatly indebted for many conversations on both the contemporary and on assemblages, I am less interested in establishing either the term assemblage or the term contemporary (with which I am much less concerned here) as technical terms than in a playful exploration of their heuristic value for thinking about how to analyze difference in time.

41. Traditionally, all of these elements were regarded as independent, as having their own line of flight. Virology, for example, has been its own field, with its own history, a history of institutions, laboratories, discoveries, experimental systems. The same is true for veterinology and public health and ornithology and the management of river courses.

42. I write "chance formulation," as Serres seems to have used the formulation in an ad hoc manner, and also because he never developed the term into a technical concept.

43. Again I want to refer here to the work of Tarek Elhaik.

Elhaik has used Rabinow's concept of the contemporary and has abstracted from it the question of what it would mean to come up with a contemporary anthropology, one that is in conversation with—that studies but also learns from—contemporary art. See especially Elhaik (2013, 2016).

44. I think of the work of Carlo Caduff and Celia Lowe, but also of Julianne Yip and Frédéric Keck. With respect to SARS see Kleinman and Watson (2005).

45. Or take in vitro fertilization in Jordan (Collier and Ong 2005). To have IVF in Jordan you need eggs and sperm—and more than a century's worth of biological research, largely with sheep (I could lift off here in an associate flight about England and Kinship and sheep and Australia and New Zealand). You also need airplanes—for bringing eggs and sperm from the United States to Jordan (and hence IVF in Egypt is contingent on a vast international aeronautics infrastructure). Why airplanes? As people in Jordan generally don't like to donate gametes, they usually come from North American college students. Consequently, you need a college population, and a biomedical infrastructure that can extract and freeze eggs and sperm (and you need advertisements, in newspapers and

on the Internet, to attract students/donors). And, critically, you need refrigerators (and, hence, electricity), which is a whole separate infrastructure project in Jordan.

IVF in Jordan is a wild, untamed assemblage of heterogeneous technologies, concepts, histories, infrastructures, knowledge, biologies, and so on (with the consequence that an instance of globalization is thus becoming visible as a heterogeneous assemblage of people and things, infrastructure and expertise and machines).

I thank Marcia Inhorn for a long discussion about the globalization of IVF and how to analyze it.

46. According to Anna Tsing (2015, 22–23): "The term assemblage is helpful. Ecologists turned to assemblages to get around the sometime fixed and bounded connotations of ecological "community." The question of how the varied species in a species assemblage influence each other—if at all—is never settled: some thwart (or eat) each other; others work together to make life possible; still others just happened to find themselves in the same place. Assemblages are open-ended gatherings. They allow us to ask about communal effects without assuming them. They show us potential histories in the making. For my purposes, however, I need to see lifeways—and non-living ways of being as well—coming together. Nonhuman ways of being, like human ones, shift historically. For living things species identities are a place to begin. But they are not enough: ways of being are emergent forms of encounters. . . . Assemblages don't just gather lifeways; they make them. Thinking through assemblages urges us to ask: How do gatherings sometimes become 'happenings,' that is, greater than the sum of their parts? If history without progress is indeterminate and multidirectional, might assemblages show us its possibilities? Patterns of unintentional coordination develop in assemblages."

Tsing offers a powerful critique of some of the ways in which the term "assemblage" has been used thus far. She writes (2015, 292–93): "Some social scientists use the term to refer to something more like a Foucaultian discursive formation (e.g., Aihwa Ong and Stephen Collier, eds., Global Assemblages). Such 'assemblages' expand across space and conquer place; they are not constituted through indeterminacy. Because constitutive encounters are a key for me, my assemblages are what gathers in a place, at whatever scale. Other 'assemblages' are networks, as in Actor-Network-Theory (Latour, *Reassembling the Social*). A network is a chain of associations that structures further associations; my assemblages gather ways of being without assuming that interactional structure."

While I share Tsing's differentiation of assemblages from ANTs, I don't share her critique of Collier's and Ong's use of the term as planned and thus intentional or human (as the example of IVF in Jordan shows, there might be some degree of planning, but I think that no amount of planning can exhaust the indeterminacy of the assemblage).

47. Why then not just rely on the dispositif? Because, as Paul Rabinow (2003) has observed, a dispositif is a combination of elements—of concepts and practices and institutions and infrastructures—that is relatively stable over a relatively long period of time, and as such it is not a good concept—or model—for analyzing the continuous lines of flight of elements and how they relate to and enable each other, especially not where the relations are fickle and/or fragile.

48. Though one could also refer here to Kuhn's (1962) paradigm shift or to the often-used term "revolution" (Shapin 1996).

49. Wherever such a claim is made, one enters murky water. Is the shift really as radical as one claims? Haven't there been earlier formations that undermine one's claim?

50. The goal of an anthropology of difference in time should not be predetermined as the study of an event that divides a scene in a before and an after—but rather as an inquiry into movement (which then might be a rupture).

51. Calhoun (2010), Redfield (2013).

52. Rees (2014a, 2015), Brown et al. (2006).

53. For a related—in my reading complementary—anthropology of the present as a temporal figuration that doesn't rely on the assemblage concept, see Kath Weston's *Gender in Real-Time* (2002). And for Weston's elaborations on what "real-time" means in an interview with Stefan Helmreich, see Weston and Helmreich 2006. See as well the fascinating new book by Nikolai Ssorin-Chaikov, *The Two Lenins* (2017).

54. The question is hardly arbitrary.

"I have come to think," John Borneman (2007, xii) recently wrote, "that the quality of writing as well as our interpretative skills has been compromised by subsuming all listening, viewing, observation, interaction, comparison, and contextualization into historical narratives."

To Borneman, the subjection of anthropology to history—think of it as the subjection of anthropology to genealogy—amounts to one big loss: "Lost is the accidental, incidental, and occasional; the serendipitous, fateful, and irregular; events and scenes that don't always hang together, that resist facile inclusion in a temporal development or argument. Lost is the episodic: experience that is personal, tied to a particular time and place, a part that does not always readily fit into the whole" (Borneman 2007, xii).

On the one hand, I want to celebrate Borneman's list: the accidental, incidental, occasional, serendipitous. Borneman brings into view the role and relevance chance plays in anthropological, especially fieldwork-based, knowledge production. On the other hand, I find myself vehemently disagreeing with Borneman. For several different reasons. First, I am critical of Borneman's critique of the present in terms of an imagined past: as if anthropological texts of the pre-1990s or pre-1980s were so rich in listening, viewing, observation, interaction, comparison, and, above all, episode. Is it necessary to put the present down? Second, I think Borneman's depiction of history is grossly inadequate. As if historiography were devoid of the serendipitous, the irregular, of episodes, of scenes and events that don't hang together and resist facile inclusion in a temporal development or argument. And third, I have a vague impression that Borneman confuses history or historical modes of inquiry with an anthropology interested in difference in time.

55. As Foucault noted in *The Order of Things* (1973): some *future* event will make the formation crumble. See as well Rabinow's (2003).

ON THE ACTUAL (RATHER THAN THE EMERGENT)

1. I am grateful to Stefan Helmreich and Mette Nordahl Svendson for conversations about the difference between the actual and the potential or potentialities. See the special edition of *Current Anthropology* 54 (7) from October 2013, which contains an essay that emerged from a Wenner-Gren Symposium, "The Anthropology of Potentiality in Biomedicine."

2. The phrase "anthropology of the actual" was first used by Rabinow (2003, 55), who uses the "actual" synonymous with "the recent past and the near future." For Rabinow the term indicates the time span of his anthropology of the contemporary, which itself is modeled on Foucault's history of the present: Where Foucault's history of the present is concerned with the long histories that gave rise to the present, the anthropology of the contemporary is concerned with the recent past/near future a.k.a. the actual (for example, when Foucault writes that Kant was concerned with "la pure actualité," the English has that Kant was concerned with "contemporary reality alone"). In a later work, Rabinow and Stavrinakis (2013, 11), the term actual is used to mark a difference between the present (still largely used in a Foucauldian sense) and the actual (still used in the sense of a distinctive analytical focus on a recent past/near future).

My use of the term, while indebted to Rabinow, differs significantly. What concerns me is not a Foucault indebted anthropology of the here and now but the effort to make plausible a form of research—an almost artistic investigation understood as (virtuous) exercise—that renders visible the irreducibly open. To that end, or this is my aim in this chapter, I try to invent a rich, differentiating vocabulary that makes visible a sensibility rarely displayed.

3. At stake is also no genealogy of the actual, nor the construction of a tradition that one would wish to hold up. As far as I can see, there never really was any reflective effort to elaborate the concept of the actual in order to open up a space of inquiry.

4. I assemble these bits and pieces from works that themselves did not evolve around—perhaps did not even mention—the idea of the concept of the actual, not in any coherent, nor in any conceptually reflective, way.

5. The English version goes (Foucault 1984, 34): "He deals with contemporary reality alone."

6. Foucault offered his reading of Kant as an elaboration of his own work. Kant's work, he seemed to say, consistently evolved around the effort to think of the present as an exit, and the form this search for an exit took was to bring into view his present's pure actuality.

7. The idea of a "rupture" was first presented by Bachelard as a correction of the naïveté of the assumption of a linear progress of truth/knowledge. See particularly his *Essai sur la connaissance approchée* (1927) and his *Étude sur l'évolution d'un problème de physique: La propagation thermique dans les solides* (1928). The idea of a fundamental discontinuity between everyday notions of reality—as informed by philosophy—was first articulated by Bachelard in his *Le nouvel esprit scientifique* (1934). See as well his *La formation de l'esprit scientifique* (1938).

8. The French original goes: "Les trajectoires qui permettent de séparer les isotopes dans les spectroscopes de masse n'existent pas dans la nature; il faut les produire techniquement. Elles sont de théorème reifiés" (Bachelard 1949, 103).

9. New categories of thought were needed—not for all times but for each new experiment. In his later work Bachelard referred to his efforts to understand the contemporary state of the human mind through the history of science as "rational materialism" (1953) or as "applied rationalism" ([1949] 1966).

10. Canguilhem (2005).

11. At stake, Canguilhem (2005, 53) adds, is "die neuen Zeiten nachzuleben, die Zeiten, in denen gerade die wissenschaftlichen Fortschritte allenthalben explodieren und so die traditionelle Epistemologie notwendig sprengen."

In my translation: At stake is "to relive the new times, that is, the times in which scientific progress everywhere makes huge leaps and thereby necessarily explodes the traditional epistemology."

12. Some of these region-specific ruptures will merely reconfigure an already established concept, others will perhaps generate a new concept, breaking open a novel epistemological region. If you wish, they lack any sense of the epochal.

13. See especially Deleuze's book on Bergson, *Le Bergsonisme* (1966).

14. It cannot provide—and does not aspire to provide—"scalable knowledge" (Tsing 2015).

Likewise, the anthropology of the actual is not much concerned with concept work. While it studies concepts in motion, it doesn't itself aspire to invent general concepts—condensations of the particular into the universal—that could then guide future research. If it is interested in concept work at all, then, insofar as its focus on conceptual motion makes it wonder about how to conceptually capture that which escapes that motion.

15. It is unlikely that such anecdotes produce any coherent picture of the open—or of the new formation that might or might not emerge. Unlikely and also irrelevant. Unlikely, for if the open (the actual) does not exist except in bits and pieces, in fleeting, fugitive formations, which might or might not stabilize—then there isn't factually any necessary coherence (or order). Irrelevant, for the aim is not to capture the new successor formation but rather something of the actual, that is, of the open that reigns before the motion has given rise to a new possible.

16. Put differently, the challenge is to practice what I called "an analysis of movement in terms of movement." "Of movement"—insofar as the being set in motion of concepts (which may result in their breaking open) is the focus of one's research. "In terms of movement"—insofar as the way to capture movement is to expose the concepts we have and to then map if, and if, then how, precisely, they are set in motion.

17. Such "enabling anecdotes" put a fieldworker—an anthropologist—in a position to give contour, by way of precise fieldwork-based description, not to what new possible is emerging but to the play of movement itself, to how the old order falls apart and how its elements are in motion.

18. If the actual cannot be captured in the abstract—if it does not exist in the abstract, as pure movement—but only in relation to words and things in motion, then perhaps the only way to get at the actual is fieldwork: the immersion in a concrete domain, the getting drowned in it, carried away, while staying alert to—movement.

It follows that it would be naïve—wrong—to assume that one could abstract *the* actual from scenes of nonteleological movement, as if behind a given conceptual formation one could find *the* real. On the contrary, there is no single *the* actual. Each one is different, perhaps even incommensurable with any other one.

19. And knowledge?

The anthropology of the actual does not shy away from producing knowledge—or from an interest in truth. However, the knowledge it produces—the kind of truth it tries to get a hold of—does not refer to any stable, object-like formation "out there." Neither does it describe the rise of a category of knowledge, nor can the movements it seeks to capture be subsumed under any existing category of knowledge. Rather its knowledge comes in forms of recognitions, of openings, of surprises, of discoveries; it does not seek to generate generalities with which one could, eventually, build the house of truth; instead it seeks to keep things moving.

20. I thank Miriam Ticktin for many conversations about the detection of the actual as a political mode of action.

21. Note that I am speaking here not about anthropology as such—but about an anthropology interested in the actual.

22. To refer to Guattari and Deleuze (1994, 5) again: if the goal is to capture something of the always new, then poetry is the genre.

I add that Fiamm Montezemolo and Norma Jeane (and Tarek Elhaik and Marina Pugliese and David Moretti), on the one hand, and Anthony Dunn, Fiona Raby, Tim Marshall, and Jamer Hunt, on the other, convince me that the scope is broader than poetry: it is art and design (in the sense of Gestaltung).

23. Do I have to add that to speak of joy doesn't mean to say that the anthropology of the actual isn't serious? Or hard labor? That it has nothing to do with despair?

bibliography

Abu-Lughod, Lila. 1991. "Writing Against Culture." In Richard G. Fox (ed.), *Recapturing Anthropology: Working in the Present*, 137–62. Santa Fe: School of American Research Press.

Adams, Vincanne. 2013. *Markets of Sorrow, Labors of Faith: New Orleans in the Wake of Katrina*. Durham, NC: Duke University Press.

Adorno, Theodor W. 1970. *Ästhetische Theorie*. Frankfurt/Main, Germany: Suhrkamp.

Althusser, Louis. [1965] 2005. "Marxism and Humanism." In *For Marx*, 219–48. London: Verso.

Amit, Vered, ed. 2000. *Constructing the Field: Ethnographic Fieldwork in the Contemporary World*. London: Routledge.

Apollinaire, Guillaume. [1913] 1980. *Les peintres cubistes*. Paris: Éditions Hermann.

Appadurai, Arjun. 1991. "Global Ethnoscapes: Notes and Queries for a Transnational Anthropology." In *Interventions: Anthropologies of the Present*, edited by R. G. Fox, 191–210. Santa Fe, NM: School of American Research.

Appadurai, Arjun. 1995. "The Production of Locality." In *Counterwork*, edited by R. Fardon, 204–25. London: Routledge.

Appadurai, Arjun. 1996. *Modernity at Large: Cultural Dimensions of Globalization*. Minneapolis: University of Minnesota Press.

Arendt, Hannah. 1958. *The Human Condition*. Chicago: The University of Chicago Press.

Asad, Talal, ed. 1973. *Anthropology and the Colonial Encounter*. London: Ithaca Press.

Bachelard, Gaston. 1927. *Essai sur la connaissance approchée*. Paris: Vrin.

Bachelard, Gaston. 1928. *Étude sur l'évolution d'un problème de physique: La propagation thermique dans les solides*. Paris: Vrin.

Bachelard, Gaston. 1934. *Le nouvel esprit scientifique*. Paris: Presses Universitaires de France.

Bachelard, Gaston. 1938. *La formation de l'esprit scientifique: Contribution à une psych-analyse de la connaissance objective*. Paris: Vrin.

Bachelard, Gaston. 1953. *Le matérialisme appliqué*. Paris: Presses Universitaires de France.

Bachelard, Gaston. [1949] 1966. *Le rationalisme appliqué*. Paris: Presses Universitaires de France.

Bastian, Adolf. 1895. *Ethnische Elementargedanken in der Lehre vom Menschen*. Berlin: Weidmann.

Bayly, Christopher A. 2003. *The Birth of the Modern World, 1780–1914: Global Connections and Comparisons*. Oxford: Blackwell.

Bergson, Henri. 1946. *The Creative Mind: An Introduction to Metaphysics*. Translated by M. L. Andison. New York: The Philosophical Library.

Bergson, Henri. 2015. *Denken und schöpferisches Werden: Aufsätze und Vorträge*. Frankfurt am Main, Germany: Europäische Verlagsanstalt.

Bessire, Lucas and David Bond. 2014. "Ontological anthropology and the deferral of critique." *American Ethnologist* 41 (3): 440–56.

Bessire, Lucas and David Bond. 2014. "The Ontological Spin," https://culanth.org /fieldsights/494-the-ontological-spin.

Biehl, João. 2007. *Will to Live: AIDS Therapies and the Politics of Survival*. Princeton, NJ: Princeton University Press.

Biehl, João. 2011. "Having and Idea in Anthropology Today." Koeber Anthropological Society Papers, vol. 99/100.

Boellstorff, Tom. 2016. "For Whom the Ontology Turns: Theorizing the Digital Real." *Current Anthropology* 57 (4): 387–407.

Borneman, John. 2007. *Syrian Episodes: Sons, Fathers, and an Anthropologist in Aleppo*. Princeton, NJ: Princeton University Press.

Brandt, Reinhard. 2014. *Die Bestimmung des Menschen bei Kant*. Hamburg, Germany: Felix Meiner.

Brown, Theodore M., Marcos Cueto, and Elizabeth Fee. 2006. "The World Health Organization and the Transition from 'International' to 'Global' Public Health." *American Journal of Public Health* 96 (1): 62–72.

Bunzl, Matti. 2004. "Boas, Foucault, and the 'Native Anthropologist': Notes toward a Neo-Boasian Anthropology," *American Anthropologist* 106 (3): 435–42.

Bunzl, Matti. 2005. "Anthropology Beyond Crisis." *Anthropology and Humanism* 30 (2): 187–95.

Bunzl, Matti. 2008. "The Quest for Anthropological Relevance: Borgesian Maps and Epistemological Pitfalls." *American Anthropologist* 110 (1): 53–60.

Burckhardt, Jacob. 1930. *Die Kultur der Renaissance in Italien*. Stuttgart, Germany: Deutsche Verlags-Anstalt.

Butler, Judith. 2002. "What Is Critique? An Essay on Foucault's Virtue." In *The Political: Readings in Continental Philosophy*, edited by D. Ingram, 212–26. London: Basil Blackwell.

Caduff, Carlo. 2010. "Public Prophylaxis: Pandemic Influenza, Pharmaceutical Prevention and Participatory Governance." *BioSocieties* 5 (2): 199–218.

Caduff, Carlo. 2015. *The Pandemic Perhaps: Dramatic Events in a Public Culture of Danger*. Oakland: University of California Press.

Candea, Matei. 2007. "Arbitrary Locations: In Defense of the Bounded field Site." *J.R.A.I*, no. 13 (1): 167–84.

Calhoun, Craig. 2010. "The Idea of Emergency: Humanitarian Action and Global

(Dis)order." In *Contemporary States of Emergency: the Politics of Military and Humanitarian Interventions*, edited by F. Didier and M. Pandolfi, 29–58. New York: Zone Books.

Callon, Michel. 1998. "An Essay on Framing and Overflowing: Economic Externalities Revisited by Sociology." *Sociological Review* 46 (S1): 244–69.

Callon, Michel. 2013. "Qu'est-ce qu'un agencement marchand?" In *Sociologie des agencements marchands: Textes choisis*, edited by M. Callon et al., 325–440. Paris: Presses des Mines.

Canguilhem, Georges. 1994. *Etudes d'histoire et de philosophie des sciences concernant les vivants et la vie*. Paris: Vrin.

Canguilhem, Georges. 2000. *La connaissance de la vie*. Paris: Vrin.

Canguilhem, Georges. 2005. "The Object of the History of Science." In *Continental Philosophy of Science*, edited by Gary Cutting, 157–75. London: Wiley Blackwell.

Cerwonka, Allaine, and Liisa Malkki. 2007. *Improvising Theory: Process and Temporality in Ethnographic Fieldwork*. Chicago, IL: University of Chicago Press.

Chakrabarty, Dipesh. 2000. *Provincializing Europe: Postcolonial Thought and Historical Difference*. Princeton, NJ: Princeton University Press.

Cheung, Tobias. 2008. "Regulating Agents, Functional Interactions, and Stimulus-Reaction-Schemes: The Concept of 'Organism' in the Organic System Theories of Stahl, Bordieu, and Barthes." *Science in Context* 110 (1): 495–519.

Clifford, James, and George E. Marcus, eds. 1986. *Writing Culture: The Poetics and Politics of Ethnography*. Berkeley: University of California Press.

Clifford, James. 1988. The Predicament of Culture. Twentieth Century Ethnography, Literature, and Art. Cambridge, MA: Harvard University Press.

Cohen, Lawrence. 1999. *No Aging in India: Alzheimer's, The Bad Family, and Other Modern Things*. Berkeley: University of California Press.

Cohen, Lawrence. 2001. "The Other Kidney: Biopolitics Beyond Recognition." *Body and Society* 7 (2–3): 9–29.

Coleman, E. Gabriella. 2013. *Coding Freedom: The Ethics and Aesthetics of Hacking*. Princeton, NJ: Princeton University Press.

Collier, Stephen J. 2011. *Post-Soviet Social: Neoliberalism, Social Modernity, Biopolitics*. Princeton, NJ: Princeton University Press.

Collier, Jane Fishburne, and Sylvia Junko Yanagisako. 1987. *Gender and Kinship: Essays Toward a Unified Analysis*. Stanford, CA: Stanford University Press.

Cook, James. 1967. *The Journals of Captain James Cook on His Voyage of Discovery: The Voyage of the Resolution and Discovery, 1776–1780: Part 1 to 3*. Cambridge: Cambridge University Press.

Crane, Peter. 2013. *Ginkgo: The Tree That Time Forgot*. New Haven, CT: Yale University Press.

Crapanzano, Vincent. 1980. *Tuhami: Portrait of a Moroccan*. Chicago, IL: University of Chicago Press.

Das, Veena. 1996. "Language and Body: Transactions in the Construction of Pain." In *Social Suffering*, edited by A. Kleinman et al., 67–91. Berkeley: University of California Press.

Das, Veena, Michael D. Jackson, et al. 2014. *The Ground Between: Anthropologists Engage Philosophy*. Durham, NC: Duke University Press.

Daston, Lorraine, and Fernando Vidal, eds. 2004. *The Moral Authority of Nature*. Chicago, IL: University of Chicago Press.

DeLanda, Manuel. 2006. *A New Philosophy of Society: Assemblage Theory and Social Complexity*. New York: Continuum.

Deleuze, Gilles. 1966. *Le Bergsonisme*. Paris: Presses Universitaires de France.

Deleuze, Gilles, and Claire Parnet. [1977] 2007. *Dialogues 2*. Translated by H. Tomlinson and B. Habberjam. New York: Columbia University Press.

Deleuze, Gilles, and Félix Guattari. 1980. *Mille plateaux*. Paris: Éditions de Minuit.

Deleuze, Gilles, and Félix Guattari. 1987. *Thousand plateaus*. Translated by Brian Massumi. Minneapolis: University of Minnesota Press.

Deleuze, Gilles, and Félix Guattari. 1994. *What Is Philosophy?* Translated by G. Burchell and H. Tomlinson. London: Verso.

Descola, Philippe. 1996a. "Constructing Natures: Symbolic Ecology and Social Practice." In *Nature and Society: Anthropological Perspectives*, edited by P. Descola and G. Pálsson, 82–102. London: Routledge.

Descola, Philippe. 1996b. *In the Society of Nature: A Native Ecology in Amazonia*. Translated by N. Scott. Cambridge: Cambridge University Press.

Descola, Philippe. 2010a. "Anthropologie de la nature." *Annuaire du Collège de France, 2008–2009: Résumé des cours et travaux 109e année* 109:521–38.

Descola, Philippe. 2010b. *Diversité des natures, diversité des cultures*. Paris: Bayard Culture.

Descola, Philippe. 2013. *Beyond Nature and Culture*. Translated by J. Lloyd. Chicago, IL: University of Chicago Press.

Descola, Philippe. 2014. "Modes of Being and Forms of Predication." *HAU: Journal of Ethnographic Theory* 4 (1): 271–80.

Dewey, John. 1993. *How We Think*. Boston, MA: D. C. Heath.

Diderot, Denis. 1755. "Encyclopédie." In *Encyclopédie, ou dictionnaire raisonné des sciences, des arts et des métiers*, Vol. 5:635–49. edited by D. Diderot and Jean le Rond d'Alembert. Paris: Le Breton, Durand, Briasson, Michel-Antoine David.

Durkheim, Émile. 1893. *De la division de travail social*. Paris: Félix Alcan.

Durkheim, Émile. 1895. *Les règles de la methode sociologique*. Paris: Félix Alcan.

Durkheim, Émile. 1897. *Le suicide*. Paris: Félix Alcan.

Durkheim, Émile. 1912. *Les formes élémentaires de la vie religieuse*. Paris: Alcan.

Durkheim, Émile, and Marcel Mauss. 1902. "De quelques formes primitives de classification: Contribution à l'étude des représentations collectives." *L'Année Sociologique* 1901–2:1–72.

Durkheim, Émile, and Marcel Mauss. 1963. *Primitive Classification*. Chicago, IL: University of Chicago Press.

Dwyer, Kevin. 1982. *Moroccan Dialogues: Anthropology in Question*. Baltimore, MD: Johns Hopkins University Press.

Edwards, Jeanette, Sarah Franklin, et al. 1999. *Technologies of Procreation: Kinship in the Age of Assisted Conception*. 2nd ed. London: Routledge.

Eggan, Fred, and W. Lloyd Warner. 1956. "Alfred Reginal Radcliffe-Brown, 1881–1955." *American Anthropologist* 58 (3): 544–47.

Elhaik, Tarek. 2013. "What Is Contemporary Anthropology?" *Critical Arts* 27 (6): 784–98.

Elhaik, Tarek. 2016. *The Incurable-Image: Curating Post-Mexican Film and Media Arts.* Edinburgh: Edinburgh University Press.

Elhaik, Tarek, and George E. Marcus. 2010. "Curatorial Designs in the Poetics and Politics of Ethnography Today: Conversation between Tarek Elhaik and George E. Marcus." In *Beyond Ethnographic Writing* (English edition), edited by A. Forero and L. Simeone, 177–94. Rome: Armando Publishers.

Evans-Pritchard, Edward Evan. 1929. "The Morphology and Function of Magic: A Comparative Study of Trobriand and Zande Ritual and Spells." *Bulletin of the Faculty of Arts* (Fuad I University, Cairo) 1/2:1–21; republished in *Journal of the Anthropological Society of Oxford* 4 (1973): 123–42.

Evans-Pritchard, Edward Evan. 1933. "The Intellectualist (English) Interpretation of Magic." *Bulletin of the Faculty of Arts* (Fuad I University, Cairo) 1/2: 1–21.

Evans-Pritchard, Edward Evan. 1937. *Witchcraft, Oracles and Magic among the Azande.* Oxford: Oxford University Press.

Evans-Pritchard, Edward Evan. 1940. *The Nuer: A Description of the Modes of Livelihood and Political Institutions of a Nilotic People.* Oxford: Clarendon Press.

Fabian, Johannes. 1983. *Time and the Other: How Anthropology Makes Its Object.* New York: Columbia University Press.

Fanon, Frantz. 1961. *Les damnés de la terre.* Paris: Éditions Maspero.

Fassin, Didier, ed. 2012. *A Companion to Moral Anthropology.* Oxford: Wiley-Blackwell.

Fassin, Didier, ed. 2014. "The Parallel Lives of Anthropology and Philosophy." In *The Ground Between: Anthropologists Engage Philosophy*, edited by V. Das et al., 50–70. Durham, NC: Duke University Press.

Ferguson, James. 2010. "The Uses of Neoliberalism." *Antipode* 41 (S1): 166–84.

Ferguson, James. 2013a. "Declarations of Dependence: Labor, Personhood, and Welfare in Southern Africa." *Journal of the Royal Anthropological Institute* 19 (2): 223–42.

Ferguson, James. 2013b. "How to Do Things with Land: A Distributive Perspective on Rural Livelihoods in Southern Africa." *Journal of Agrarian Change* 13 (1): 166–74.

Ferguson, James. 2015. *Give a Man a Fish: Reflections on the New Politics of Distribution.* Durham, NC: Duke University Press.

Firth, Raymond. 1929. *Primitive Economics of the New Zealand Maori.* London: Routledge.

Firth, Raymond. 1936. *We, the Tikopia: A Sociological Study of Kinship in Primitive Polynesia.* London: George Allen & Unwin.

Fischer, Hans. 1970. "'Völkerkunde,' 'Ethnographie,' 'Ethnologie': Kritische Kontrolle der frühesten Belege. Zeitschrift für Ethnologie." Band 95, Heft 2: 169–82.

Fischer, Michael J. 1999. "Emergent Forms of Life: Anthropologies of Late or Postmodernities." *Annual Review of Anthropology* 28:455–78.

Fischer, Michael J. 2004. *Mute Dreams, Blind Owls, and Dispersed Knowledges: Persian Poesis in the Transnational Circuitry.* Durham, NC: Duke University Press.

Flaubert, Gustave. 1913. *Le dictionnaire des idées reçues.* Paris: Éditions Conrad.

Foley, Douglas. 2011. "Review of Rabinow et al. Designs for an Anthropology of the Contemporary." *Collaborative Anthropologies* 4:276–86.

Formoso, Bernard. 2011. "Review of Rabinow et al. Designs for an Anthropology of the Contemporary." *L'Homme*, no. 194:181–83.

Fortes, Meyer. 1945. *The Dynamics of Clanship among the Tallensi: Being the First Part of an Analysis of the Social Structure of a Trans-Volta Tribe.* London: International African Institute/Oxford University Press.

Foucault, Michel. [1966] 1990. *Les mots et les choses: Une archéologie des sciences humaines.* Paris: Gallimard.

Foucault, Michel. 1969. *L'archéologie du savoir.* Paris:: Éditions Gallimard.

Foucault, Michel. 1970. *L'ordre du discours.* Paris: Flammarion.

Foucault, Michel. 1972. *The Archaeology of Knowledge.* London: Routledge.

Foucault, Michel. 1973. *The Order of Things: An Archaeology of the Human Sciences.* New York: Vintage Press.

Foucault, Michel. 1980. *Power/Knowledge: Selected Interviews and Other Writings, 1972–1977.* New York: Pantheon Books.

Foucault, Michel. 1984. "What Is Enlightenment?" In *The Foucault Reader*, edited by P. Rabinow, 32–50. New York: Pantheon Books.

Foucault, Michel. 1985. *The Use of Pleasure, Vol. 2, The History of Sexuality.* Translated by R. Hurley. New York: Vintage Books.

Foucault, Michel. 2008a. *Introduction to Kant's Anthropology.* Translated by R. Nigro and K. Briggs. Semiotext(e).

Foucault, Michel. 2008b. *The Birth of Biopolitics. Lectures at the College du France 1978–79.* New York: Palgrave McMillan.

Franklin, Sarah. 1997. *Embodied Progress: A Cultural Account of Assisted Conception.* London: Routledge.

García, Andrés, and Julien Cossette. 2016. "Election's Reverb: An Interview with Stefan Helmreich." *Cultural Anthropology: Fieldsights.* Accessed March 9, 2017. https://culanth.org/fieldsights/1011-election-s-reverb-an-interview-with-stefan-helmreich.

Gardner, Brian. 1971. *The East India Company: A History.* London: Rupert Hard-Davis.

Geertz, Clifford. 1973. *The Interpretation of Cultures.* New York: Basic Books.

Gellner, Ernest. 1998. *Language and Solitude: Wittgenstein, Malinowski and the Habsburg Dilemma.* Cambridge: Cambridge University Press.

Geroulanos, Stefanos. 2010. *An Atheism That Is Not Humanist Emerges in French Thought.* Stanford: Stanford University Press.

Gupta, Akhil, and James Ferguson, eds. 1997a. *Locations: Boundaries and Grounds of a Field Science.* Berkeley: University of California Press.

Gupta, Akhil, and James Ferguson, eds. 1997b. *Culture, Power, Place: Explorations in Critical Anthropology.* Durham, NC: Duke University Press.

Gusterson, Hugh. 1996. *Nuclear Rites: A Weapons Laboratory at the End of the Cold War.* Berkeley: University of California Press.

Hacking, Ian. 1986. "Making Up People." In *Reconstructing Individualism: Autonomy, Individuality, and the Self in Western Thought*, edited by T. C. Heller et al., 222–36. Stanford, CA: Stanford University Press.

Hacking, Ian. 2004. *Historical Ontology*. Cambridge, MA: Harvard University Press.

Haddon, Alfred Cort. 1895. *Evolution in Art*. London: Walter Scott.

Haddon, Alfred Cort. 1935. *General Ethnography*. Vol. 1, *Reports of the Cambridge Anthropological Expedition to Torres Straits*. Cambridge: Cambridge University Press.

Haddon, Alfred Cort, and W. H. R. Rivers. 1912. *Arts and Crafts, Vol. 4, Reports of the Cambridge Anthropological Expedition to Torres Straits*. Cambridge: Cambridge University Press.

Haddon, Alfred Cort, W. H. R. Rivers, et al. 1904. *Sociology, Magic and Religion of the Western Islanders, Vol. 5, Reports of the Cambridge Anthropological Expedition to Torres Straits*. Cambridge: Cambridge University Press.

Handler, Richard. 1991. "An Interview with Clifford Geertz." *Current Anthropology* 32 (5): 603–13.

Haraway, Donna J. 1990. *Primate Visions: Gender, Race, and Nature in the World of Modern Science*. New York: Routledge.

Haraway, Donna J. 1991. "A Cyborg Manifesto: Science, Technology, and Socialist-Feminism in the Late Twentieth Century." In *Simian, Cyborgs, and Women: The Reinvention of Nature*, 149–81. New York: Routledge.

Haraway, Donna J. 1997. *Modest_Witness@Second_Millennium.FemaleMan©Meets _OncoMouse™: Feminism and Technoscience*. New York: Routledge.

Haraway, Donna J. 2003. *The Companion Species Manifesto: Dogs, People, and Significant Otherness*. Chicago, IL: Prickly Paradigm Press.

Haraway, Donna J. 2008. *When Species Meet*. Minneapolis: University of Minnesota Press.

Haraway, Donna J. 2016. *Staying with the Trouble: Making Kin in the Chthulucene*. Durham, NC: Duke University Press.

Haraway, Donna J., Noboru Ishikawa, et al. 2016. "Anthropologists Are Talking—About the Anthropocene." *Ethnos* 81 (3): 535–64.

Harbsmeier, Michael. 1985. "On Travel Accounts and Cosmological Strategies: Some Models in Comparative Xenology." *Ethnos* 50 (3–4): 273–312.

Hayden, Cori. 2000. *When Nature Goes Public: The Making and Unmaking of Bioprospecting in Mexico*. Berkeley: University of California Press.

Hegel, Georg Wilhelm Friedrich. [1820] 1991. *Elements of the Philosophy of Right*. Trans. A. W. Wood and ed. H. B. Nisbet. Cambridge: Cambridge University Press.

Heidegger, Martin. [1938] 1950. *Die Zeit des Weltbildes*. In *Holzwege*, 69–104. Frankfurt, Germany: Klostermann.

Heidegger, Martin. [1927] 2006. *Sein und Zeit*. Berlin: De Grutyer.

Heidegger, Martin. 1977. "The Age of the World Picture." In *The Question Concerning Technology and Other Essays*. New York: Harper and Row.

Helmreich, Stefan. 2003. "Trees and Seas of Information: Alien Kinship and the Biopolitics of Gene Transfer in Marine Biology and Biotechnology." *American Ethnologist* 30 (3): 340–58.

Helmreich, Stefan. 2009. *Alien Ocean: Antropological Voyage in Microbial Seas*. Berkeley: University of California Press.

Helmreich, Stefan. 2014. "The Water Next Time: Changing Wavescapes in the Anthropocene." Paper presented at the Center for 21st Century Studies, University of Wisconsin-Milwaukee, April 4.

Helmreich, Stefan. 2015. *Sounding the Limits of Life: Essays in the Anthropology of Biology and Beyond*. Princeton, NJ: Princeton University Press.

Herder, Johann Gottfried von. 1774. *Auch eine Philosophie der Geschichte zur Bildung der Menschheit*. Riga, Latvia: 1. Auflage.

Holbraad, Martin. 2009. "Ontology, Ethnography, Archaeology: An Afterword on the Ontography of Things." *Cambridge Archaeological Journal* 19 (3): 431–41.

Holbraad, Martin, Morton Axel Pedersen, and Eduardo Viveiros de Castro. 2014. "The Politics of Ontology: Anthropological Positions." *Cultural Anthropology: Fieldsights*. Accessed February 4, 2018. https://culanth.org/fieldsights/462-the-politics-of-ontology-anthropological-positions.

Hyde, Sandra Teresa. 2007. *Eating Spring Rice: The Cultural Politics of AIDS in Southwest China*. Berkeley: University of California Press.

Hymes, Dell H. 1974. *Reinventing Anthropology*. New York: Vintage Books.

Ingold, Tim. 2011. *Being Alive: Essays on Movement, Knowledge, and Description*. London: Routledge.

Ingold, Tim. 2014. "That's enough about ethnography." In: *HAU: Journal of Ethnographic Theory* 4 (1): 383–95.

Ingold, Tim. 2016. "Enough about Ethnography: An Interview with Tim Ingold." https://culanth.org/fieldsights/841-enough-about-ethnography-an-interview-with-tim-ingold (Accessed on February 6, 2018): 1–7.

Ingold, Tim. 2017. "Anthropology contra ethnography." In: *HAU: Journal of Ethnographic Theory* 7 (1): 21–26.

Kant, Immanuel. 1902. *Kants gesammelte Schriften*. Edited by Königlich Preussische Akademie der Wissenschaften. Berlin: G. Reimer.

Keay, John. 1991. *The Honourable Company: A History of the English East India Company*. London: Harper Collins.

Keck, Frédéric. 2008. *Lucien Lévy-Bruhl, entre philosophie et anthropologie: Contradiction et participation*. Paris: Editions du CNRS 2010.

Keck, Frédéric. 2010. *Un monde grippé*. Paris: Flammarion.

Keen, W. W. 1897. "Address in Surgery." Delivered at the Semi-Centennial Meeting of the American Medical Association at Philadelphia, PA, June 3, 1897. *JAMA*, 28 (24): 1102–10.

Kelty, Christopher M. 2008. *Two Bits: The Cultural Significance of Free Software*. Durham, NC: Duke University Press.

Kelty, Christopher M. 2009. "Conceiving Open Systems." *Washington University Journal of Law and Policy* 30:139–77.

Kirksey, S. Eben. 2012. "Living with Parasites in Palo Verde National Park." *Environmental Humanities* 1 (1): 23–55.

Kirksey, S. Eben. 2014. *The Multispecies Salon*. Durham, NC: Duke University Press.

Kirksey, S. Eben, and Stefan Helmreich. 2010. "The Emergence of Multispecies Ethnography." *Cultural Anthropology* 25 (4): 545–76.

Kleinman, Arthur. 1988. *The Illness Narratives: Suffering, Healing, and the Human Condition*. New York: Basic Books.

Kleinman, Arthur, and James L. Watson, eds. 2005. *SARS in China: Prelude to Pandemic?* Stanford, CA: Stanford University Press.

Kleinman, Arthur, Veena Das, and Margaret M. Lock, eds. 1997. *Social Suffering.* Berkeley: University of California Press.

Kohn, Eduardo. 2007. "How Dogs Dream: Amazonian Natures and the Politics of Transspecies Engagement." *American Ethnologist* 34 (1): 3–24.

Kohn, Eduardo. 2013. *How Forests Think: Toward an Anthropology Beyond the Human.* Berkeley: University of California Press.

Kohn, Eduardo. 2015. "Anthropology of Ontologies." *Annual Review of Anthropology* 44:311–27.

Koselleck, Reinhardt. 1979. *Vergangene Zukunft: Zur Semantik geschichtlicher Zeiten.* Frankfurt am Main, Germany: Suhrkamp.

Koselleck, Reinhardt. 2000. *Zeitschichten. Studien zur Historik.* Frankfurt am Main, Germany: Suhrkamp.

Koselleck, Reinhardt. 2002. *The Practice of Conceptual History: Timing, History, Spacing Concepts (Cultural Memory in the Present).* Stanford, CA: Stanford University Press.

Koselleck, Reinhardt. 2006. *Begriffsgeschichten.* Frankfurt am Main, Germany: Suhrkamp.

Koselleck, Reinhardt. 2010. *Vom Sinn und Unsinn der Geschichte: Aufsätze und Vorträge aus vier Jahrzehnten.* Berlin: Suhrkamp.

Kramer, Fritz. 1977. *Verkehrte Welten: Zur imaginaren Ethnographie des 19. Jahrhundert.* Frankfurt, Germany: Syndikat.

Kramer, Fritz. 2005. *Schriften zur Ethnographie.* Frankfurt am Main: Suhrkamp.

Kramer, Fritz and Gertraud Marx. 1993. *Zeitmarkern: Die Feste von Dimodonko.* München: Trickster.

Krauss, Werner. 2011. "Review of Rabinow et al. Designs for an Anthropology of the Contemporary." *American Ethnologist* 36 (1): 187–90.

Kropotkin, Peter. [1902] 1909. *Mutual Aid: A Factor of Evolution.* New York: Doubleday.

Kuhn, Thomas. 1962. *The Structure of Scientific Revolutions.* Chicago, IL: University of Chicago Press.

Kuklick, Henrika. 1991. *The Savage Within: The Social History of British Anthropology, 1885–1945.* Cambridge: Cambridge University Press.

Kuper, Adam, ed. 2010. *The Social Anthropology of Radcliffe-Brown.* London: Routledge.

Landecker, Hannah. 2000. "Immortality, In Vitro: A History of the HeLa Cell Line." In *Biotechnology and Culture: Bodies, Anxieties, Ethics,* edited by P. E. Brodwin, 53–74. Bloomington: Indiana University Press.

Landecker, Hannah. 2002. "New Times for Biology: Nerve Cultures and the Advent of Cellular Life in Vitro." *Studies in History and Philosophy of Biological and Biomedical Sciences* 33:667–94.

Landecker, Hannah. 2010. *Culturing Life: How Cells Became Technologies.* Cambridge, MA: Harvard University Press.

Langlitz, Nicolas. N.d. "Primatology of Science: A Right-Latourian Reading of Actor-Network Theory and the Prosocial Turn in the Behavioral Sciences." Unpublished manuscript.

Latour, Bruno. 1987. *Science in Action: How to Follow Scientists and Engineers through Society*. Cambridge, MA: Harvard University Press.

Latour, Bruno. 1988. *The Pasteurization of France*. Translated by A. Sheridan and J. Law. Cambridge, MA: Harvard University Press.

Latour, Bruno. 1991. *Nous n'avons jamais été modernes: Essai d'anthropologie symétrique*. Paris: La Découverte.

Latour, Bruno. 1993. *We Have Never Been Modern*. Cambridge, MA: Harvard University Press.

Latour, Bruno. 1999. *Pandora's Hope: Essays on the Reality of Science Studies*. Cambridge, MA: Harvard University Press.

Latour, Bruno. [1999] 2004. *The Politics of Nature: How to Bring the Sciences into Democracy*. Translated by C. Porter. Cambridge, MA: Harvard University Press.

Latour, Bruno. 2005. *Reassembling the Social: An Introduction to Actor-Network-Theory*. Oxford: Oxford University Press.

Law, John, and Marianne Elisabeth Lien. 2013. "Slippery: Field Notes in Empirical Ontology." *Social Studies of Science* 43 (3): 363–78.

Lawson, Philip. 2014. *The East India Company: A History*. London: Routledge.

Leclerc, Gerard. 1972. *Anthropologie et colonialisme*. Paris: Payot.

Levinas, Emmanuel. 1981. *Otherwise than Being, or Beyond Essence*. Translated by A. Lingis. The Hague: Martinus Nijhoff.

Lévi-Strauss, Claude. 1962. *Le totemisme aujourd'ui*. Paris: Universitaires de France.

Lévy-Bruhl, Lucien. 1894. *La philosophie de Jacobi/* Paris: Félix Alcan.

Lévy-Bruhl, Lucien. 1910. *Les fonctions mentales dans les sociétés inférieurs*. Paris: Félix Alcan.

Lévy-Bruhl, Lucien. 1922. *La mentalité primitive*. Paris: Félix Alcan.

Lévy-Bruhl, Lucien. 1926. *How Natives Think*. London: Allen & Unwin.

Lévy-Bruhl, Lucien. 1952. "A Letter to E. E. Evans-Pritchard." *British Journal of Sociology* 3 (2): 117–23.

Lewis, Diane. 1973. "Anthropology and Colonialism." *Current Anthropology* 14 (5): 581–602.

Lichtblau, Klaus. 1996. *Kulturkrise und Soziologie um die Jahrhundertwende*. Frankfurt am Main: Suhrkamp.

Lin, Keh-Ming, and Arthur M. Kleinman. 1988. "Psychopathology and Clinical Course of Schizophrenia: A Cross-Cultural Perspective." *Schizophrenia Bulletin* 14 (4): 555–67.

Lock, Margaret M. 1993. *Encounters with Aging: Mythologies of Menopause in Japan and North America*. Berkeley: University of California Press.

Lock, Margaret M., and Deborah Gordon, eds. 1988. *Biomedicine Examined*. Dordrecht, Germany: Kulwer Academic.

Lowe, Celia. 2010. "Viral Clouds: Becoming H5N1 in Indonesia." *Cultural Anthropology* 25 (4): 625–49.

Lynch, Michael. 2013. "Ontography: Investigating the Production of Things, Deflating Ontology." *Social Studies of Science* 43 (3): 444–62.

Malinowski, Bronisław. [1922] 2005. *Argonauts of the Western Pacific*. London: Routledge.

Marcus, George E. 1986. "Contemporary Problems of Ethnography in the World System." In *Writing Culture. The Poetics and Politics of Ethnography*, edited by Georges Marcus and James Clifford, 165–92. Berkeley: University of California Press.

Marcus, George E. 1995. "Ethnography in/of the World System: The Emergence of Multi-Sited Ethnography." *Annual Review of Anthropology* 24:95–117.

Marcus, George E. 1998. *Ethnography through Thick and Thin*. Princeton, NJ: Princeton University Press.

Marcus, Georges, and James Clifford. 1986. *Writing Culture. The Poetics and Politics of Ethnogrpahy*. Berkeley: University of California Press.

Marcus, George E., and Michael M. J. Fischer. 1986. *Anthropology as Cultural Critique: An Experimental Moment in the Human Sciences*. Chicago, IL: University of Chicago Press.

Marquard, Odo. 1973. *Schwierigkeiten mit der Geschichtsphilosophie*. Frankfurt am Main, Germany: Suhrkamp.

Martin, Emily. 1987. *The Woman in the Body: A Cultural Analysis of Reproduction*. Boston, MA: Beacon Press.

Masco, Joseph. 2006. *The Nuclear Borderlands: The Manhattan Project in Post–Cold War New Mexico*. Princeton, NJ: Princeton University Press.

Masco, Joseph. 2014. *The Theater of Operations*. Durham, NC: Duke University Press.

Maurer, Bill. 2005. "Introduction to Ethnographic Emergences." *American Anthropologist*, 107 (1): 1–4.

Mauss, Marcel. 1931. "La Cohésion sociale dans les sociétés polysegmentaires. Communication présentée à l'Institut français de sociologie." *Bulletin de l'Institut Français de Sociologie*, I, 49–68.

Mauss, Marcel. [1938] 1950. "Une Catégorie de l'esprit humain: la notion de personne, celle du 'moi.'" In *Sociologie et Anthropologie*. Paris: Presses Universitaires de France.

Mauss, Marcel. [1931] 1950. "Débat sur les rapports entre la sociologie et la psychologie." In *Sociologie et Anthropologie*. Paris: Presses Universitaires de France.

Mazzarella, William. 2013. *Censorium: Cinema and the Open Edge of Mass Publicity*. Durham, NC: Duke University Press.

McLennan, John Ferguson. 1865. *Primitive Marriage. An Inquiry into the Origins of the form of Capture in Marriage Ceremonies*. Edinburgh: Adam & Charles Black.

McLennan, John Ferguson. 1877. *Studies in Ancient History*. London, New York: McMillan and Co.

Messeri, Lisa. 2016. *Placing Outer Space: An Earthly Ethnography of Other Worlds*. Durham: Duke University Press.

Mol, Annemarle. 2002. *The Body Multiple. Ontology in Medical Practice*. Durham, NC: Duke University Press.

Morgan, Lewis Henry. 1871. *Systems of Consanguinity and Affinity of the Human Family*. Washington: Smithsonian Institute.

Morgan, Lewis Henry. 1877. *Ancient Society. Or Researches in the Lines of Human of Progress from Savagery through Barbarism to Civilization*. New York: Henry Holt and Company.

Nguyen, Vinh-Kim. 2014. "Ebola: How We Became Unprepared, and What Might Come Next. *Cultural Anthropology: Fieldsights*. Accessed March 7, 2016. https://culanth.org /fieldsights/605-ebola-how-we-became-unprepared-and-what-might-come-next.

Norrmann, Gerhard Philipp Heinrich. 1785. *Geographisches und Historisches Handbuch der Länder-, Völker-und Staatenkunde*. 5 Bde: Hamburg, Germany: B.G. Hoffmann.

Ong, Aihwa, and Stephen J. Collier, eds. 2005. *Global Assemblages: Technology, Politics, and Ethics as Anthropological Problems*. Malden, MA: Blackwell Publishing.

Ortega y Gasset, José. 1962. *La deshumanización del arte*. Madrid: Revista del Ocidente.

Osterhammel, Jürgen. 2009. *Die Verwandlung der Welt: Eine Geschichte des 19. Jahrhunderts*. Munich, Germany: C. H. Beck.

Paleček, Martin, and Mark Risjord. 2013. "Relativism and the Ontological Turn within Anthropology." *Philosophy of the Social Sciences* 43 (1): 3–23.

Pandian, Anand. 2012. "The Time of Anthropology: Notes from a Field of Contemporary Experience." *Cultural Anthropology* 27 (4): 547–71.

Pandian, Anand. 2015. *Reel World: An Anthropology of Creation*. Durham, NC: Duke University Press.

Paxson, Heather. 2008. "Post-Pasteurian Cultures: The Microbiopolitics of Raw-Milk Cheese in the United States." *Current Anthropology* 23 (1): 15–47.

Paxson, Heather. 2012. *The Life of Cheese: Crafting Food and Value in America*. Berkeley, CA: University of California Press.

Petryna, Adriana. 2002. *Life Exposed: Biological Citizens after Chernobyl*. Princeton, NJ: Princeton University Press.

Petryna, Adriana. 2009. *How Experiments Travel*. Princeton, NJ: Princeton University Press.

Peukert, Detlev. 1987. *Die Weimarer Republik: Krisenjahre der klassischen Moderne* [The Weimar Republic: The crisis of modernity]. Frankfurt, Germany: Suhrkamp.

Philips, C. H. 1961. *The East India Company, 1784–1834*. Manchester, UK: Manchester University Press.

Phillips, John. 2006. "Agencement/Assemblage." *Theory, Culture and Society* 23 (2–3): 108–9.

Pollan, Michael. 2001. *The Botany of Desire: A Plant's-Eye View of the World*. New York: Random House.

Poktonjak, Sanja. 2010. "Review of Rabinow et al. Designs for an Anthropology of the Contemporary." *Etnoloska Tribina* 40 (33): 143–45.

Ponte, Alessandra. 2014. *The House of Light and Entropy*. London: Architectural Association, School of Architecture.

Povinelli, Elizabeth A. 2014. "Geontologies of the Otherwise." *Cultural Anthropology: Fieldsights*. Accessed February 4, 2018. https://culanth.org/fieldsights/465-geontologies-of-the-otherwise.

Povinelli, Elizabeth A. 2016. *Geontologies: A Requiem to Late Liberalism*. Durham, NC: Duke University Press.

Powdermaker, Hortense. 1933. *Life in Lesu: The Study of Melanesian Society in New Ireland*. New York: The Norton Library.

Quetelet, Adolphe. 1829. "Recherches sur la population, les naissances, les décès, les prisons, les dépôts de mendicité, etc., dans le royaume des Pays-Bas." *Nouveaux*

Mémoire de l'Académie Royale des Sciences et Belles Lettres de Bruxelles, vol. 4, 115–65.

Quetelet, Adolphe. 1835. *Sur l'homme et le développement de ses facultés, ou Essai de physique sociale*. 2 vols. Paris: Bachelier.

Quetelet, Adolphe. 1848. "Sur la statistique morale et les principes qui doivent en former la base." *Mémoires de l'Académie Royale des Sciences, des Lettres et des Beaux-Arts de Belgique*, vol. 29:1–68

Rabinow, Paul. 1986. "Representations Are Social Facts: Modernity and Post-Modernity in Anthropology." In *Writing Culture: The Poetics and Politics of Ethnography*, edited by J. Clifford and G. E. Marcus, 234–61. Berkeley: University of California Press.

Rabinow, Paul. 1989. *French Modern: Norms and Forms of the Social Environment*. Cambridge, MA: MIT Press.

Rabinow, Paul. 1996a. *Essays on the Anthropology of Reason*. Princeton, NJ: Princeton University Press.

Rabinow, Paul. 1996b. *Making PCR: A Story of Biotechnology*. Chicago, IL: University of Chicago Press.

Rabinow, Paul. 1999a. "Epilogue: The Anthropological Contemporary." In *French DNA: Trouble in Purgatory*, 167–82. Chicago, IL: University of Chicago Press.

Rabinow, Paul. 1999b. *French DNA: Trouble in Purgatory*. Chicago, IL: University of Chicago Press.

Rabinow, Paul. 2002. "Midst Anthropology's Problems." *Cultural Anthropology* 17 (2): 135–49.

Rabinow, Paul. 2003. *Anthropos Today: Reflections on Modern Equipment*. Princeton, NJ: Princeton University Press.

Rabinow, Paul. 2008. *Marking Time: On the Anthropology of the Contemporary*. Princeton, NJ: Princeton University Press.

Rabinow, Paul. 2017. *Unconsolable Contemporary. Observing Gerhard Richter*. Durham: Duke University Press.

Rabinow, Paul, George E. Marcus, et al. 2008. *Designs for an Anthropology of the Contemporary*. Durham, NC: Duke University Press.

Radcliffe-Brown, Alfred Reginald. 1922. *The Andaman Islanders: A Study in Social Anthropology*. Cambridge: Cambridge University Press.

Radin, Paul. 1927. *Primitive Man as Philosopher*. New York: D. Appleton.

Radin, Paul. 1998. "Two Letters to Edward Sapir." *History of Anthropology Newsletter* 25 (1): 4–7.

Radin, Paul. [1933] 1965. *The Method and Theory of Ethnology: An Essay in Criticism*. New York: Basic Books.

Raffles, Hugh. 2011. *Insectopedia*. New York: Vintage Books.

Rapp, Rayna. 1988. "Chromosomes and Communication: The Discourse of Genetic Counseling." *Medical Anthropology Quarterly* 2 (2): 143–57.

Rapp, Rayna. 1990. "Constructing Amniocentesis: Medical and Maternal Voices." In *Uncertain Terms: Negotiating Gender in America*, edited by F. Ginsburg and A. Tsing, 28–42. Boston, MA: Beacon Press.

Redfield, Peter. 2013. *Life in Crisis: The Ethical Journey of Doctors Without Borders*. Berkeley: University of California Press.

Rees, Tobias. 2010a. "To Open Up New Spaces of Thought: Anthropology BSC (Beyond Society and Culture)." *Journal of the Royal Anthropological Institute* 16 (1): 158–63.

Rees, Tobias. 2010b. Being Neurologically Human Today: Life, Science, and Adult Cerebral Plasticity (An Ethical Analysis)." *American Ethnologist* 37 (1): 150–66.

Rees, Tobias. 2011. "As if Theory is the only Form of Thinking and Social Theory the only Form of Critique," in: *Dialectical Anthropology* 35 (3): 341–65.

Rees, Tobias. 2014a. "Humanity/Plan; or, On the 'Stateless' Today (Also Being an Anthropology of Global Health)." *Cultural Anthropology* 29 (3): 457–78.

Rees, Tobias. 2014b. "Snails, Subjects, and Suffering: An Anthropology of (Neuro)Biology." A paper presented at the conference "End of Biodeterminism? New Directions for Medical Anthropology," Aarhus, Denmark, October 1.

Rees, Tobias. 2015a. "On Global Health and Humanity. An Interview with Tobias Rees." https://culanth.org/fieldsights/745-tobias-rees-on-global-health-and-humanity.

Rees, Tobias. 2015b. "Developmental Diseases: An Introduction to the Neurological Human (in Motion)." *American Ethnologist* 42 (1): 161–74.

Rees, Tobias. 2015c. "Once Cell Death, Now Cell Life. On Plasticity and Pathology ca. 1800 to 2014." In: David Bates Nima Bassri (eds.), *Plasticity and Pathology*, Bronx: Fordham University Press.

Rees, Tobias. 2016. *Plastic Reason. An Anthropology of Brain Science in Embryogentic Terms*. Oakland: UC Press.

Reyes, Angela. 2014. "Linguistic Anthropology in 2013: Super-New-Big." *American Anthropologist* 116 (2): 366–78.

Rheinberger, Hans-Jörg. 2010. *An Epistemology of the Concrete: Twentieth-Century Histories of Life*. Durham, NC: Duke University Press.

Richards, Audrey I. 1932. *Hunger and Work in a Savage Tribe: A Functional Study of Nutrition among the Southern Bantu*. London: George Routledge & Sons.

Rivers, W. H. R. 1900. "A Genealogical Method of Collecting Social and Vital Statistics." *Journal of the Anthropological Institute of Great Britain and Ireland*, Vol. 30, 74–82.

Rivers, W. H. R. 1906. *The Todas*. London: MacMillan.

Rivers, W. H. R. 1910. "The Genealogical Method of Anthropological Inquiry." *Sociological Review* 3 (1): 1–12.

Rivers, W. H. R. 1912. "A General Account of Method." In *Notes and Queries on Anthropology*. 4th ed. London: Routledge and Kegan Paul.

Rivers, W. H. R. 1922. *History and Ethnology*. London: Society for Promoting Christian Knowledge.

Roitman, Janet. 2014. *Anti-Crisi*. Durham, NC: Duke University Press.

Roosth, Sophia. "Screaming Yeast: Sonocytology, Cytoplasmic Milieus, and Cellular Subjectivities." *Critical Inquiry* 35 (2): 332–50.

Rosaldo, Renato. 1980. *Ilongot Headhunting, 1883–1974: A Study in Society and History*. Stanford, CA: Stanford University Press.

Rousseau, Jean-Jacques. 1750. *Discours sur les sciences et les arts*. Geneva: Bartillot et Fils.

Rousseau, Jean-Jacques. 1755. *Discours sur l'origine et les fondements de l'inégalité parmi les hommes.* Amsterdam: Marc Michel Rey.

Said, Edward. 1978. *Orientalism.* New York: Pantheon Books.

Salazar, Noel B. 2009. Review of Rabinow, Paul, George E. Marcus, James D. Faubion & Tobias Rees 2008 Designs for an Anthropology of the Contemporary." *Anthropology Review Database.*

Schapera, Isaac. 1930. *The Khoisan Peoples of South Africa.* London: Routledge.

Schapera, Isaac. 1938. *A Handbook of Tswana Law and Custom.* Oxford: Oxford University Press.

Scheper-Hughes, Nancy. 1992. *Death without Weeping: The Violence of Everyday Life in Brazil.* Berkeley: University of California Press.

Schlich, Thomas. 2016. "'One and the Same the World Over': The International Culture of Surgical Exchange in an Age of Globalization, 1870–1914." *Journal of the History of Medicine and Allied Sciences* 71 (3): 247–70.

Scholte, Bob. 1974. "Toward a Reflexive and Critical Anthropology." In *Reinventing Anthropology,* edited by Dell Hymes, 430–58. Ann Arbor: University of Michigan Press.

Schneider, David Murray. 1995. "Studying Kinship." In *Schneider on Schneider: The Conversion of the Jews and Other Anthropological Stories.* 193–218. Durham, NC: Duke University Press.

Seligman, Charles G. 1910. *The Melanesians of British New Guinea.* Cambridge: Cambridge University Press.

Seligman, Charles G. 1930. *Races of Africa.* London: Thornton Butterworth.

Seligman, Charles G., and Brenda Z. Seligman. 1911. *The Veddas.* Cambridge: Cambridge University Press.

Seligman, Charles G., and Brenda Z. Seligman. 1932. *Pagan Tribes of the Nilotic Sudan.* London: George Routledge & Sons.

Serres, Michel. 1995. "Second Conversation: Method." In *Conversations on Science, Culture, and Time,* edited by Michael Serres and Bruno Latour, 43–77. Ann Arbor: University of Michigan Press.

Serres, Michael, and Bruno Latour, eds. 1995. *Conversations on Science, Culture, and Time.* Ann Arbor: University of Michigan Press.

Shapin, Steven. 1996. *The Scientific Revolution.* Chicago: University of Chicago Press.

Snell, Bruno. 1946. *Die Entdeckung des Geistes: Studien zur Entstehung des europäischen Denkens bei den Griechen.* Hamburg, Germany: Claassen & Goverts.

Snell, Bruno. 1960. *The Discovery of the Mind: The Greek Origins of European Thought.* Translated by T. G. Rosenmeyer. New York: Harper and Row.

Spivak, Gayatri Chakravorty. 1987. *In Other Worlds: Essays in Cultural Politics.* London: Methuen.

Spivak, Gayatri Chakravorty. 1990. *The Post-Colonial Critic: Interviews, Strategies, Dialogues.* London: Routledge.

Ssorin-Chaikov, Nikolai. 2017. *Two Lenins. A Brief Anthropology of Time.* Chicago: The University of Chicago Press.

Stagl, Justin. 1995. *A History of Curiosity: The Theory of Travel, 1550–1800.* Chur: Harwood Academic Publishers.

Stahl, Georg Ernst. 1695. *Disputatio inauguralis de Passionibus Animi Corpus Humanum varie alterantibus.* Halle: Christian Henckel.

Stanner, William Edward Hanley. 1969. *After the Dreaming (The 1968 Boyer Lectures).* Australian Broadcasting Commission.

Stanner, William Edward Hanley. 1956. "A. R. Radcliffe-Brown." *Kroeber Anthropological Society Papers,* Vol. XIII, 116–25.

Stocking, George W., Jr. 1968. *Race, Culture, and Evolution: Essays in the History of Anthropology.* San Francisco: The Free Press.

Stocking, George W., Jr. 1987. *Victorian Anthropology.* New York: The Free Press.

Stocking, George W., Jr. 1992. *The Ethnographer's Magic and Other Essays in the History of Anthropology.* Madison: University of Wisconsin Press.

Stocking, George W., Jr. 2001. *Delimiting Anthropology: Occasional Essays and Reflections.* Madison: The University of Wisconsin Press.

Stocking, George W., Jr., ed. 1984. *Functionalism Historicized: Essays on British Social Anthopology.* Madison: The University of Wisconsin Press.

Strathern, Marilyn. 1972. *Women in Between: Female Roles in a Male World: Mount Hagen, New Guinea.* London, New York: Seminar Press.

Strathern, Marilyn. 1988. *The Gender of the Gift: Problems with Women and Problems with Society in Melanesia.* Berkeley: University of California Press.

Strathern, Marilyn. 1991. *Partial Connections.* Savage, MD: Rowman & Littlefield.

Strathern, Marilyn. 1992a. *After Nature: English Kinship in the Late Twentieth Century.* Cambridge: Cambridge University Press.

Strathern, Marilyn. 1992b. *Reproducing the Future: Essays on Anthropology, Kinship and the New Reproductive Technologies.* Manchester: Manchester University Press.

Strathern, Marilyn. 1995. *The Relation: Issues in Complexity and Scale.* Cambridge: Prickly Pear Press.

Tedlock, Dennis. 1979. "The Analogical Tradition and the Emergence of a Dialogical Anthropology." *Journal of Anthropological Research* 35:387–400.

Thomas, Nicholas. 1996. *Out of Time: History and Evolution in Anthropological Discourse.* Ann Arbor: University of Michigan Press.

Thompson, Charis. 2007. *Making Parents: The Ontological Choreography of Reproductive Technologies.* Cambridge, MA: MIT Press.

Traweek, Sharon. 1988. *Beamtimes and Lifetimes: The World of High-Energy Physicists.* Cambridge, MA: Harvard University Press.

Trujillo, Michael L. 2011. "Review of Rabinow et al. Designs for an Anthropology of the Contemporary." *Journal of Anthropological Research* 67 (3): 463–65.

Tsing, Anna L. 1993. *In the Realm of the Diamond Queen: Marginality in an Out-of-the-Way Place.* Princeton, NJ: Princeton University Press.

Tsing, Anna L. 2005. *Friction: An Ethnography of Global Connection.* Princeton, NJ: Princeton University Press.

Tsing, Anna L. 2015. *The Mushroom at the End of the World: On the Possibility of Life in Capitalist Ruins.* Princeton, NJ: Princeton University Press.

Urry, James. 1993. *Before Social Anthropology: Essays on the History of British Anthropology*. London: Routledge.

Vertesi, Janet. 2015. *Seeing Like a Rover: How Robots, Teams, and Images Craft Knowledge of Mars*. Chicago: The University of Chicago Press.

Viveiros de Castro, Eduardo. 1998. "Cosmological Deixis and Amerindian Perspectivism." *Journal of the Royal Anthropological Institute* 4 (3): 469–88.

Viveiros de Castro, Eduardo. 2004a . "Exchanging Perspectives: The Transformation of Objects into Subjects in Amerindian Ontologies." *Common Knowledge* 1 (3): 463–84.

Viveiros de Castro, Eduardo. 2004b. "Perspectival Anthropology and the Method of Controlled Equivocation." *Tipití: Journal of the Society for the Anthropology of Lowland South America* 2 (1): 3–22.

Viveiros de Castro, Eduardo. 2014. *Cannibal Metaphysics*. Minneapolis: University of Minnesota Press.

Voltaire. [1756] 1829. *Essai sur les moeurs et l'esprit des nations*. Vol. 1. Geneva: Cramer.

Voltaire. 1765. *La philosophie de l'histoire*. Amsterdam: Chez Changuion.

Wagner, Peter. 1999. "'An Entirely New Object of Consciousness, of Volition, of Thought': The Coming into Being and (Almost) Passing Away of 'Society' as a Scientific Object." In *Biographies of Scientific Objects*, edited by Lorraine Daston, 132–57. Chicago, IL: University of Chicago Press.

Wallerstein, Immanuel. 1982. *World-Systems Analysis: Theory and Methodology*. Beverly Hills, CA: Sage.

Warner, William Lloyd and Paul S. Lunt. 1941. *The Social Life of a Modern Community*. New Haven, CT: Yale University Press.

Warner, William Lloyd and Josiah Orne Low. 1947. *The Social System of the Modern Factory. The Strike: A Social Analysis*. New Haven, CT: Yale University Press.

Warner, William Lloyd and William Earl Henry. 1948. "The Radio Day Time Serial: A Symbolic Analysis." *Genetic Psychology Monographs* 37:3–71.

Warner, William Lloyd. 1949a. *Democracy in Jonesville: A Study of Quality and Inequality*. New York: Harper & Row.

Warner, William Lloyd. 1949b. *Social Class in America: A Manual of Procedure for the Measurement of Social Status*. Gloucester, MA: P. Smith.

Welsch, Wolfgang. 2011. *Immer nur der Mensch? Entwürfe zu einer anderen Anthropologie*. Berlin: Akademie Verlag.

Weston, Kath. 1991. *Families We Choose: Lesbians, Gays, Kinship*. New York: Columbia University Press.

Weston, Kath. 2002. *Gender in Real Time: Power and Transience in a Visual Age*. New York: Routledge.

Weston, Kath. 2017. *Animate Planet: Making Visceral Sense of Living in a High-Tech Ecologically Damaged World*. Durham: Duke University Press.

Weston, Kath and Stefan Helmreich. 2006. "Kath Weston's Gender in Real Time. Power and Transience in a Visual Age. Kath Weston Interviewed by Stefan Helmreich." *Body & Society* 12 (3): 103–21.

Wynter. Sylvia. 2000. "The Re-Enchantment of Humanism: An Interview with Sylvia Wynter." *Small Axe*, 8:119–207.

Wynter. Sylvia. 2015. *Sylvia Wynter: On Being Human as Praxis.* Durham: Duke University Press.

Wolf, Eric. 1982. *Europe and the People Without History.* Berkeley: University of California Press.

Woolf, Virginia. 1938. *Three Guineas.* London: Hogarth Press.

Woolgar, Steve, and Javier Lezaun. 2013. "The Wrong Bin Bag: A Turn to Ontology in Science and Technology Studies?" *Social Studies of Science* 43 (3): 321–40.

Wurgaft, Benjamin Aldes. 2015. *Thinking in Public: Strauss, Levinas, Arendt.* Philadelphia: University of Pennsylvania Press.

Young, Allan. 1997. *The Harmony of Illusions: Inventing Post-Traumatic Stress Disorder.* Princeton, NJ: Princeton University Press.

Young, Michael. 2004. *Malinowski: Odyssey of an Anthropologist, 1884–1920.* New Haven, CT: Yale University Press.

Zammito, John H. 2002. *Kant, Herder, and the Birth of Anthropology.* Chicago, IL: University of Chicago Press.

index

Hume, David, 36, 39
Hyde, Sandra, 88

ice, 12, 43, 132n22, 25n133
Ingold, Tim, 124n27, 133n28, 135n42
insects, 44, 55, 123n22. *See also* Raffles, Hugh
irreducible open(ness), 26, 32, 41, 44, 103,
    131n20

James, William, 21

Kant, Immanuel, 36, 38–40, 98, 129nn13–16,
    148n2
Keck, Frédéric, 145n44
Kelty, Cristopher, 79, 123n21
Kirksey, S. Eben, 55–56
Kleinman, Arthur, 22, 122n11
knowledge, 24, 38, 50, 57, 100, 103–4, 112,
    136nn45–46, 149–50n19
Kohn, Eduardo, 56, 59–60, 64–66, 137n55
Koselleck, Reinhardt, 129n10
Kramer, Fritz W., 95, 125n25, 138n56, 141n20
Kropotkin, Peter, 140n19

Landecker, Hannah, 79
Langer, Susan, 126n30
Langlitz, Nicolas, 48, 79
language, 21, 78
Latham, Robert, 73
Latour, Bruno, 10, 53, 55, 58–62, 65, 84, 134n31,
    135–36n44, 136nn48–50, 137n52, 146n46
Law, John, 55, 60
Leclerc, Gerard, 95
Levinas, Emmanuel, 21, 67
Levi-Strauss, Claude, 20, 29
Lévy-Bruhl, Lucien, 7, 17, 19–20, 28–29,
    126n30
Lewis, Diane, 95
Lock, Margaret, 122n11, 127n35
logos, 45, 47
Lowe, Celia, 79, 123n21, 145n44

Maine, Henry, 73
making up people, 45, 134n29
Malherbe, François de, 129n11

Man, 2, 16, 34, 100, 118, 128n1, 131n19
man, 22–23, 123n23
Marcus, George, 143–44n34; and Clifford,
    James, 121n2, 121nn8–9, 122n10, 123n20
Mars, 133n26
Maupertius, Pierre, Louis, 129n11
Mauss, Marcel, 7, 18–20, 126n28, 137n53,
    140n19
McDougall, William, 75
McLennon, John, 73, 140n16
Mead, Margaret, 12, 40
meaning, 1–2, 13, 23, 35, 37–39, 64, 78, 155–56,
    123n18,
Mensch, 13, 123n19, 129–30n15
MERS (Middle East respiratory syndrome), 88
Messeri, Lisa, 133n26
methane, 43, 133n25
microbes, 43, 58–59, 61, 79, 135n44, 136n48
mind, 18–19, 21, 99–100, 126n30, 148n9
modernism, 28, 30–31, 66. *See also* modernity;
    moderns
modernity, 11–12, 25, 65, 127n32, 130n15,
    145n40. *See also* moderns
moderns, 9–12, 17, 19, 31, 56, 60, 62–64, 66.
    See also modernism; modernity
Mol, Annemarie, 55, 57–62, 136n46, 136n49,
    137n52
Mondrian, Piet, 128n46
Montaigne, Michel de, 127n38
Montezemolo, Fiamma, 144n34, 150n22
morality, 5, 11, 66–67, 125n27. *See also* anthro-
    pology, moral
Morgan, Lewis Henry, 140n16
Movement, 65, 90, 102–7; of movement/
    in terms of movement, 41–44, 54, 65, 82, 87,
    108–9, 120, 132n20, 133n27, 149n16, 149n18
Müller, Friedrich, 73
multispecies. *See* anthropology, multispecies
mushroom, 44, 55
mutation, 91, 95, 120

nature, 2, 5, 14, 36–37, 47, 63, 107, 129n11;
    moral authority of, 66
nature/culture, 48, 55–56, 59–60, 65, 88, 107,
    134n3, 135n44
nature-cultures, 59, 134n31, 135n44. *See also*
    actor-network theory (ANT); nature/culture

neoliberalism, 107; city planning 12, 79; neoliberal social, 48, 133n25, 133n27, 143n33
new/different, 32, 52, 60, 108–9, 120, 143n33;
always new, 54, 104, 112, 150n19
Nguyen, Vinh-Kim, 133n25
Nietzsche, Friedrich, 29, 131n19
nonhumans, 46, 48, 55–56, 62, 64, 69, 88, 103,
132n23, 135n43, 137n55, 146n46
nonteleological, the, 44, 65, 103, 105, 112
Normann, Gerhard Philipp Heinrich, 71
not-knowing, 26

ontology, 55–69
open, the, 15, 44, 51, 53, 66, 81, 101–3, 106,
135n40, 149n15; irreducible open, 32, 82, 148n2
Ortega y Gasset, 131n19

Pandian, Anand, 80
Parnet, Claire, 67
Pasteur, Louis, 58–59, 61
Paxson, Heather, 48, 55, 79
performance, theory, 52, 136n49
Petryna, Adriana, 79
philosophy, 39, 67, 97, 102, 123n19, 127n32,
129–30n15, 130n16; and anthropology, 17,
21–23; empirical, 24, 29, 82; philosophy/
Philosophy, 25–27, 111
plants, 55, 62, 64, 67, 87, 133n25, 137n55
Pliny, 127n38
poetry, poetic, 26, 112, 114, 150n22
politics, 26, 95, 107, 112, 114, 115–17, 128n2,
130n15
Pollan, Michael, 55
Ponte, Alessandre, 138n59
post-humanism, 131n19. See also humanism
Povinelli, Elizabeth, 67, 138n57
Powdermaker, Hortense, 78, 141n25
power, 112
power/knowledge, 112, 115
practice, 58–59, 71, 112, 116–17, 143n34
precursor, 101
present, the, 14, 42, 53, 85–87, 90, 93–96, 98,
131n20, 132n22, 144n35, 147nn53–54; history
of, 145n40, 148n2
primitive, 9–11, 21, 67, 75, 78–79, 137n53,
138n56; primitive thought, 17–19,
126n30–31, 127n32

question-based. See anthropology,
question-based
Quetelet, Adolphe, 22, 53

Rabinow, Paul, 10, 45–47, 122n12, 122n14,
134n30, 145n40, 145n43, 146n47, 148n2
Radcliffe-Brown, Alfred R., 7, 12, 77, 79,
140–41n19,
Radin, Paul, 126n30, 142n28
Raffles, Hugh, 48, 55, 138n57
Ray, Sydney H., 55
reason (Vernunft), 3, 18, 25–26, 38, 100, 116
recent past, near future, 84, 145n40, 148n2
reconstruction, 73, 138n48, 144n37
relations and the relational, 31, 67–68, 76–77,
85, 87, 111, 116, 138n57, 140n15
replacement, 130n16
replacement approach, 41–42, 44, 51, 56, 65,
119, 131–32n20, 134n31
re-railment. See derailment
research: research into the open, 44, 51, 81
Rivers, William Halse Rivers, 7, 12, 28–29,
75–77, 79, 81, 136n31, 127n42, 140n15–17,
141n24
Rivet, Paul, 7
Roitman, Janet, 127n38
Rousseau, Jean Jacques, 22, 40, 129n11
rupture, 32, 50, 90–91, 99–100, 103, 124n27,
148n7. See also discontinuity

Sahlins, Marshall, 54, 126n30, 130n16
Said, Eduard, 95
Sapir, Edward, 142n28
sars (severe acute respiratory syndrome).
See severe acute respiratory syndrome
(sars)
savage, 66, 127n42, 129n11
Schapera, Isaac, 78, 141n25
Schneider, David Murray, 7, 122n17, 137n54
Scholte, Bob, 95, 121n3
science and technology studies (sts), 55, 60,
82
script, 2, 53, 125n27
Seligman, Brenda, 76
Seligman, Charles, 75–78, 139n12, 141n24
Serres, Michel, 84, 86, 144n39, 144–45n40;
contemporary and, 84, 145n49

19597930R00116

Made in the USA
Middletown, DE
06 December 2018